D1190470

PRAISE FOR
*AWAKENING THE SOUL OF POWER*

"It is a rare occurrence indeed when a book not only delivers on its message but also gives you practical, straightforward and incredibly wise ways in which to apply the teachings put forth in *Awakening the Soul of Power*. I found it to be an introspective work that is a balm for the soul of anyone searching for truth and answers to life's difficult questions, and truly look forward to the rest of Christian de la Huerta's amazing *Calling All Heroes* series. It inspired me to purchase his previous book, *Coming Out Spiritually: The Next Step*."

**—Gloria Estefan**
Singer, Songwriter, Multiple Grammy Award–Winner

"I have had the privilege of knowing Christian for over 30 years and have come to respect and admire his integrity that shines through in all that he does and attempts to do (including his breathwork, which I have profited richly from). In this book he talks about our becoming the "heroes" we are called to be. The theological word for *hero* is *saint*. The teachings and practices he lays out here are lessons appropriate to discovering holiness once again—not only our capacity for it but everyone's capacity for it. Is it time for holiness? For courage, creativity and adventure? Christian thinks so, and he offers a useful and tried map forward based on his own inner work and decades of focused retreat gatherings where life stories rise, and hearts catch fire. His is a voice worth heeding in this time of the dark night of our species."

**—Matthew Fox**
Author of *Original Blessing, The Tao of Thomas Aquinas*

"*Awakening the Soul of Power* is filled with deep ideas shared in a wonderfully playful way. Christian de la Huerta is that rare teacher who can explain serious and demanding concepts with such a light touch that we can laugh at our own foibles. He conveys so much kindness to the reader, so much acceptance and compassion,

I could feel his encouragement jumping off the pages saying "I believe in you! You can do this!" I'm so touched by his beautiful invitation to imagine what life would be like if we believed the Universe is conspiring to support us. Wow!"

**—Erica Ariel Fox**
Author of *Winning from Within*

"I have known Christian for 25 years, throughout which he has consistently offered deep healing and transformational retreats and workshops all over the world. This book, the first of a series that encapsulates his work, is clear, insightful and supportive to anyone trying to make sense of their lives and the often-subconscious ways in which we sell out on our power."

**—Chip Conley**
Hospitality Entrepreneur and Best-Selling Author

"I have known Christian for 30 years and have always been touched and inspired by his wisdom, insight and generosity. This beautiful new book is filled with clear and profound teachings, as well as practical, easy to use exercises. I'm sure it will inspire and support you to be a better you, in every area of life."

**—Marcia Wieder**
CEO, Dream University and Best-Selling Author

"Christian de la Huerta has been one of those visionaries that I believe to have a real understanding of what is called upon within each of us to make change. In his new book, *Awakening the Soul of Power,* he has created a blueprint for self-awareness that will make each of us a hero or heroine in the battle to not only change personally but in the process change the planet. Another remarkable book from a remarkable man."

**—David Mixner**
Civil Rights Activist and Author of *Stranger Among Friends*

"I know and trust Christian. During one process he led a group of us through, I had a profound experience that changed the way I think about my body, breath, and life. I'm excited for you to have this book in your hands, and for you to experience the powerful exercises in it which can change your life."

**—Dr. Clint G. Rogers**
Author of *Ancient Secrets of A Master Healer:*
*A Western Skeptic, An Eastern Master, And Life's Greatest Secrets*

"*Awakening the Soul of Power* is a beautiful invitation into self-observation and transformation—a deep dive into the psyche of why we "do what we do" and how to shift our patterns of self-limitations and false beliefs. As a fellow author and transformational coach, I would highly recommend this practical and easy to follow guide to awakening to your authentic self."

**—Jennifer Grace**
Hay House Author of *Directing Your Destiny*

"In these challenging and difficult times, Christian shows us the empowerment that lies within to be a beacon of light for others on this planet. His writing brings an increased level of self-awareness and self-honesty and allows us to integrate the disparate parts of our self. Christian's book is a heroic work that calls forth, and inspires, the true hero in each of us."

**—Brian Piergrossi**
Life Coach, Healer, Podcaster
Author of *The Big Glow* and *The Wow of the Now*

"In *Awakening the Soul of Power*, author Christian de la Huerta takes us through a transformational journey of self-discovery. Filled with inspiring quotes and powerful action steps, he summons us to shed our false ego-driven self and embrace our hidden authentic and heroic self. Thought-provoking and captivating, this is a must-read for anyone seeking to fulfill their potential!"

**—Elia Gourgouris, PhD**
Author of #1 Best-selling Book *7 Paths to Lasting Happiness*

"Timely to the point of clairvoyance, *Awakening the Soul of Power* offers a blueprint to rectify the abuses of power that plague us as individuals and as a society. It delineates how finding balance within and between us will lead to a more equitable world. Christian provides thoughtful, practical guidance for accessing our personal power and improving our lives!"

**—Terri Tate**
Author of *A Crooked Smile: A Memoir*
With foreword by Anne Lamott

"In this first book of the *Calling All Heroes* trilogy, de la Huerta offers a practical and powerful path toward profound transformation. *Awakening the Soul of Power* is not a book of mere information, a book to work on; it is a book that works on us. The promise made in the book is well kept: "Embark on it. Embrace it. Dive into it. Trust. Your heroic quest will be supported."

**—The Rev. Dr. James H. Reho**
Author of *Tantric Jesus: The Erotic Heart of Early Christianity*

"*Awakening the Soul of Power* is the real deal: a guide to personal empowerment that can truly change lives. Christian's writing style is easy and accessible, and he shares his compelling story with transparency and authenticity. But the real nugget of this series is the hands-on approach of a tangible road map through the process of personal transformation his work is designed to generate."

**—Rev. Dr. Michael Lennox**
Psychologist and Spiritual Teacher
Author of *Dream Sight*

"There is no one I know who is better suited to write this book on the healing of the soul from the tyranny of the ego than Christian de la Huerta. He's an expert, having led retreats on the subject for more than 30 years. Christian gently, fiercely, and fearlessly guides the reader inexorably into the spiritual power of their own soul. It's a book to read again and again. I can't wait for the next two of the trilogy."

**—Rev. Dr. Susan Corso**
Author of *God's Dictionary, Tao for Now,*
*Circles of Peace* and many more

"I recommend that everyone heed Christian's call to the inner adventure to explore within themselves the patterns, causes, and conflicts that hold them back from shifting into the powerful person they are at the core. We each can become the hero in our own lives to play our part in the expansion of consciousness for all."

**—Susan Harrow**
Media Coach and Marketing Strategist
Author of *Sell Yourself Without Selling Your Soul*

'I've followed Christian's career as a public speaker, conference leader, courageous activist and author for more than 30 years. This is his magnum opus, a profound work exploring his favorite theme, "the stuff of heroes." He had no idea when he began this work that an invisible virus would kill millions, bankrupt the world's economy and make us doubt all the individuals and institutions we once trusted. If ever there was a time to explore our inner hero, it is now."

**—Mel White**
Author of *Stranger at the Gate* and *Religion Gone Bad*

"Reading this book will start you on a journey of the soul. The author takes you deep into every insecurity and misconception of what heroism, safety, and power really are. He leads you out of every area where you limit yourself into something greater, not only for you, but for all. If you are lost or struggling in any area of your life, this book will give you the tools to see your path clearly. A must-read for any spiritual seeker."

**—Fay Thompson**
Access Consciousness Certified Facilitator Spiritual Coach
Author of *So Help Me God*
Editor-in-Chief Big Moose Publishing

"When in your lifetime have you seen more possibility of true change in our world of estrangement? When more have we needed to be heroic in our interactions with ourselves and others? I've known Christian for many years, and he's the real deal. If you're looking for someone to help you take the hero's journey to self-realization, let him gently, lovingly, wisely guide you. He has me."

—**Brian McNaught**
Author of *The Lincoln Chronicles: Puppy Wisdom for Happy Living*
Educator on LGBTQ+ Issues

"Christian de la Huerta's powerful and illuminating book, *Awakening the Soul of Power*, is an uncompromising study on what it means to live heroically in the world. De la Huerta inspires us to step into our spiritual heroism by taking meticulous inventory of our inner world and deep responsibility for every action that we take. He leaves no stone unturned in helping the reader to examine all the ways in which the inherent foibles of the human being can keep us from stepping into the miraculousness of our potential, and he offers many powerful practices that teach us how to develop the hero within."

—**Jonathan Hammond**
Author of *The Shaman's Mind: Huna Wisdom to Change Your Life*

"This extraordinary, life-changing book is a roadmap to respond to the call to be our full selves in the best way possible for the good of all beings and this amazing planet. It is a very important contribution to our personal and our collective healing and evolution, and it is just part one!"

—**Edward Schreiber, TEP**
Zerka Moreno Foundation
Editor of *The Quintessential Zerka*

"It's a wonderful feeling to read a book that's written to help you, where you feel the author's passion bursting from within to achieve that goal. Christian leads you through stages. He gives you the background, asks questions, and provides practical solutions—so you're not overwhelmed and don't quit before you prove to yourself that you can. Read this book, commit to the power practices, and your life can transform."

—**Robert Christiansen Ashford**
Author of *Your Inspiration Is Needed*

# Awakening the Soul of Power

## How to Live Heroically and Set Yourself Free

### Christian de la Huerta

AWAKENING THE SOUL OF POWER

© 2020 by Christian de la Huerta
All rights reserved.

Printed in the United States of America

Published by Soulful Hero Media
3191 Grand Avenue, #331763
Miami, FL 33133
www.SoulfulHeroMedia.com

All rights reserved. This book contains material protected under International and Federal Copyright Laws and Treaties. Any unauthorized reprint or use of this material is prohibited. No part of this book may be reproduced or transmitted in any form or by any means, electronic or mechanical, including photocopying, recording, or by any information storage and retrieval system, without express written permission from the author.

Library of Congress Control Number: 2020909197
ISBN: 978-1-7350590-0-6 (Hardback)
ISBN: 978-1-7350590-1-3 (Paperback)
ISBN: 978-1-7350590-2-0 (E-book)
Available in paperback, hardback, e-book, and audiobook

Book design by JetLaunch
Cover design by Lizaa
Cover art by Bruce Rolff
Author photo by Marta Neira

# CONTENTS

## PART 1. PREPARING FOR THE JOURNEY

## PART 2. THE EMPIRE OF THE EGO

# PART 3. THE ZONE OF POWER

# PART 4. DECONSTRUCTING OUR RELATIONSHIP TO POWER

# PART 5. PATHS TO SOULFUL POWER

# ILLUSTRATIONS

Oscar Paludi:

Map of the Hero's Journey
Map of the Empire of the Ego
Map of the Zone of Power
The Extreme SeeSaw

Maicol Arango:

The Ego
The Healed Ego

# PREFACE

Dear Reader:

I hope you enjoy Book 1 in my *Calling All Heroes* series.

Completing this book has probably been a journey of ten years, but really, a lifetime. Of course, I wasn't writing or actively working on it during all that time, but thinking about, conceiving the teachings, letting them brew, testing them out in retreats, putting them into practice myself.

So here we are. Finally. And not a moment too soon! What a world we now live in! Interestingly, the book's message is more timely now than ever. I've been saying "All hands on deck!" for years and calling people forth to living heroically. Guess what? We're here. The time many of us suspected would come. No more time for getting ready or getting yet one more certification before stepping into our roles as teachers and healers (however we express that). Time to rise to our highest potential. To go beyond what we thought was possible. Even remaining centered, calm, and positive amid the insanity of our collective crises is nothing short of heroic.

These are not hypothetical, theoretical, woo-woo teachings. They will require some inner work, but the rewards are priceless. Freedom. Ultimately, that's what we're talking about.

The teachings work. They helped me transform from a shy, inhibited individual stifled by self-doubt, to an undaunted, unwavering, internationally recognized authority and expert.

These days, no matter the details and circumstances of my life, I no longer question my self-worth. Never.

I do still tend to resist writing. For me, it's a long, solitary process and an intense one because I am committed to walking my talk, which means that I not only stand for everything I write about in these pages but also practice these teachings personally. Daily.

*Awakening the Soul of Power* will help you discover and unleash the hero inside of you. And yes, there is one. I promise. I know. As I just alluded to, I am an unlikely person to be writing about heroism and personal empowerment.

This book will change your life in profound and positive ways, especially if you take the time to slow down and engage with the Power Practices—the hero tasks in each chapter. This will help you embody the teachings and integrate them into your life. To make them real and practical and transform your life. If you long for personal freedom, relationships that work and a life filled with meaning and purpose, I truly believe this series will help you accomplish those things.

A couple of notes. You'll notice I alternate gender pronouns. He/she gets boring and tedious. Also, retreat participant names have been changed to protect the privacy of individuals. Finally, I chose to use the word *hero* generically for all. *Heroine* smacks of something else, and as a lover of words, I just can't go there with "shero." Forgive me. In its original Greek or in Latin or any of the modern romance languages, the "he" in *hero* has nothing to do with gender.

When you've finished reading, I'd really appreciate it if you'd take a couple of minutes to leave a review on Amazon and other online retailers. (It's easy—even a sentence or two is enough.) In today's online publishing world, reader reviews can make a real difference and contribute to a book's success. Your posting a review may just make a difference in someone's life—and will be deeply appreciated. Of course, be honest. It's okay to offer constructive criticism. I promise I will read every one of them.

Will you help spread the word? Imagine the effect in the world of 1,000,000 Soulful Heroes—all practicing and living these teachings—by 2025 and 5,000,000 by 2030.

I love hearing from readers. You can contact me directly through my website www.SoulfulPower.com. For support on the journey and community with other Soulful Heroes, join the free Facebook Group: Unleash Your Inner Hero.

Be a hero, your own kind of hero. How will you express heroism in your own life?

Much love and countless blessings on your journey!

Christian

# Awakening the Soul of Power

## How to Live Heroically and Set Yourself Free

# PART I

## PREPARING FOR THE JOURNEY

# CHAPTER 1
## WE ARE THE HELP!

We live in scary times. Plagues erupt and propagate across the globe. Fire rains down from the sky in the form of bombs, drones, and guided missiles. Terrorists detonate their bodies in public places, turn airplanes into missiles, and huddle in hidden caves plotting the demise of civilization.

Arguably, humanity is at the most critical juncture in the evolution of our species. We could even say that we are at a make-it-or-break-it point.

Our global economy is illusory, held together by Scotch tape; the entire system could come apart at any moment. We are just beginning to feel the effect our addiction to oil and carbon has had on our precious ecosystem, as droughts, superstorms, increasingly frequent earthquakes, and rising seas precipitate widespread destruction all over the planet. Big Brother reads our email, records our private phone conversations, and watches us from security cameras. All of this amplifies the feeling that we are living in apocalyptic times.

What to do? Where do we place our trust? In our political leaders? In our corruptible corporate and banking system? In our religious institutions? Those systems are no longer trustworthy. They are either frozen in impotent stalemate or facing the possibility of implosion and collapse.

To paraphrase Einstein, a problem cannot be solved from the same level of consciousness in which it was created. That means we have to think in fresh ways. As I see it, the only way we are going to free ourselves from the collective hole we have dug ourselves into is an evolutionary leap in consciousness. What we need is nothing less than a spiritual revolution.

How many more pandemics, how many more 9/11s, genocidal massacres, bombings, and mass shootings will it take for us to begin living by the values of love, generosity, and cooperation rather than fear, greed, and competition? How many more wake-up calls like Fukushima, Katrina, and Maria do we need before we reclaim a sense of connectedness to nature and to our planet?

My friend Jan Phillips, author of *The Art of Original Thinking*, tells a wonderful story about her car breaking down in the middle of Death Valley. Alone in the dark of night in a remote and desolate area, she decided to crawl under the car to see what was happening. Around a bend in the road came another car, hitting hers and pinning her under the chassis. Hardly able to move her body, she turned her head and could see two pairs of tennis shoes. A young man's voice cried out: "We gotta get help!"

Jan called back: "You are the help!"

*We* are the help.

## A TIME FOR HEROES

These times call for nothing less than heroism.

What does it mean to be a hero in the 21st century, when there are no dragons or demons to slay . . . except the ones within? And what can modern-day heroes do to midwife, catalyze, and support the necessary spiritual revolution?

We tend to associate heroism with those who display great courage and accomplish extraordinary feats or selflessly place themselves at personal risk for the sake of another being, a larger community or a cause. COVID-19 has expanded the way we view heroism to include frontline doctors, nurses, EMTs, and respiratory therapists who constantly place their lives at risk in order to help others heal and survive. Grocery store clerks, public transit operators, migrant farmworkers, and delivery people also showed up heroically in many cases, having to take extra shifts or arrange for extra childcare so they could serve the rest of us and make sure our essential needs were met. And going forward, I trust that we will develop a deeper appreciation for the often underappreciated work—measured by the way we compensate them—of our teachers. To all these heroes, thank you for your contributions to society.

What about the rest of us? During times of global pandemic or natural disasters, for example, we could argue that simply getting up in the morning, making our beds and maintaining calm, centered, and positive lives are heroic acts. Yet I feel we are being called to more. All of us. For years I've been saying "All hands on deck!" Now that time has truly come.

Presented as a three-book series, *Calling All Heroes* expands the way we think of heroism to include everyday challenges that lead to our own personal transformation and spiritual awakening, in service to humanity's evolution. In so doing, perhaps we do not place ourselves at risk of physical survival in the way a warrior hero does, but living in the ways presented here is no less heroic. Freeing ourselves from our conditioning, healing our wounds, and transcending our past traumas is an act of tremendous courage. It demands that we set aside our own needs for the greater good. It requires that we place ourselves at some degree of emotional and psychological risk. And *that* is truly the stuff of heroes.

*Calling All Heroes* is an inspiring invitation, a rousing call to unleash the courageous and powerful hero that resides inside each of us. It provides guidelines, understanding, and action steps—a viable path to living heroically in our day-to-day lives.

Below are some of the areas we will explore—all the stuff of heroes.

- The willingness to dive deep inside and face down our own inner demons, to do the challenging work of self-healing for the sake of our individual and collective liberation. Joseph Campbell and others have described the Hero's

Journey as a call to adventure. What greater adventure is there than exploring the uncharted and vast Within? That's the stuff of heroes.

- Overriding fear for the sake of personal growth and spiritual evolution, in order to achieve a better world—that's the stuff of heroes.

- Struggling with ourselves and refusing to allow the ego to keep us playing small, stuck in self-made prisons of fear and limitation—that's the stuff of heroes.

- Expanding our self-awareness in order to transcend the ego's tendencies to be right, its desire to control everyone and everything, its propensity to take everything personally—that's the stuff of heroes.

- Overriding the ego's defensiveness and learning the power of vulnerability—that's the stuff of heroes.

- Learning to tame the cruel, harsh, and ruthless inner judge that terrorizes us and others, wreaking havoc in our lives and sabotaging our dreams and relationships—that's the stuff of heroes.

- Taking the time to understand our emotional blind spots and triggers for the sake of more effective and peaceful communication in relationships—that's the stuff of heroes.

- Transcending reactivity while bringing choice back into the equation—that's the stuff of heroes.

- Being able to take the high road in interpersonal conflict through mindful, conscious self-observation—that's the stuff of heroes.

- Taking on personal accountability for all our actions and responsibility for all situations in our lives—that's the stuff of heroes.

- Refusing to be stuck in victim consciousness, in an adversarial relationship to others and to life—that's the stuff of heroes.

- Reeling in and pulling back our fantasies and projections—that's the stuff of heroes.

- Keeping our emotional heart open, no matter what. "Love your enemy" remains as radical a message today as it was 2000 years ago. The heart center cannot be closed selectively—that's the stuff of heroes.

- Refusing to be stuck in the prison of the past by forgiving even that which seems unforgivable. Forgiveness is an act of personal liberation—that's the stuff of heroes.

- Having the courage to walk away from a relationship or a job when it is clear that staying would be limiting, imprisoning, or disempowering—that's the stuff of heroes.

- Being who we are wherever we are; having the courage to be authentically and congruently ourselves to the fullest in every situation, no matter what others may think—that's the stuff of heroes.

- Pushing through laziness, risk aversion, and the desire for comfort and safety in order to step into our authentic life's purpose. Growth does not happen in the comfort zone—that's the stuff of heroes.

- Letting it rip (with compassion), no matter the consequences. The world does not need for us to hold back and play small—that's the stuff of heroes.

- Being willing to dive deep inside and face down our own inner demons: the monster of self-doubt, incapacitating fear, the possibility of failure. Heroes face overwhelming obstacles, overcome seemingly insurmountable odds, and defeat impossible enemies—that's the stuff of heroes.

- Practicing humility in a world of reality TV, a 24-hour news cycle and celebrity worship—that's the stuff of heroes.

- Finding the strength to stand alone and walk the solitary path, the road less traveled; to make tough choices for the sake of personal freedom and authentic self-expression—that's the stuff of heroes.

- Resisting fear of conflict and the pull toward appeasement and sugarcoating, committing instead to the truth and being willing to rock the boat when necessary—that's the stuff of heroes.

- Overcoming the fear of rejection and the need for acceptance that results in conformity and selling out on our true feelings and desires, stepping into our authentic power even at the risk of rejection—that's the stuff of heroes.

## SOULFUL POWER, INSPIRED LEADERSHIP

That's a formidable list, but we can accomplish them all—together. *Calling All Heroes* looks at these critical aspects of being human and provides simple, accessible tools to help understand ourselves—what makes us do the things we do and the ways in which we sabotage ourselves, our relationships, and our lives.

The first book, *Awakening the Soul of Power,* inspires readers to engage power in new ways that will ultimately generate a deeper level of fulfillment, satisfaction, and effectiveness in the world, while supporting the development of our unique expression of power congruent with our nature and values. The information imparted here will transform our relationship to power and guide us to freedom.

The other two books will be released over the next couple of years. Their working titles are:

Book 2: *Attracting and Nurturing Relationships That Work*, and
Book 3: *Living Your True Purpose and Leading with Soul.*

Sometimes in my retreats, I can almost hear the unspoken questions underlying a palpable sense of unease among the participants. All these steps toward becoming a hero can feel overwhelming, at first. Why must they step into power and leadership? How in the world can they—plumbers, housewives, doctors, office managers—answer the call for heroes? As we talk, the questions tumble out. How does a hero step into and relate to power and leadership? How does a hero navigate relationships? How does a hero negotiate livelihood and purpose?

The answer is both simple and complex:

- Because if we don't, we will shrivel up in a life of unfulfilled potential and soul-devouring mediocrity.

- Because if we don't, we will fall prey to power games, such as manipulation and passive-aggression. We'll find ourselves stuck in a self-made prison of victim consciousness.

- Because the way we embody, express, and relate to power impacts every area of our lives: work, politics, religion, personal relationships—the area in which most of us tend to forfeit our inner power.

From a larger perspective, we must answer this call because the world needs us as heroes—and soulful leaders—fully in our power. It needs everyone—all of us who have even an inkling or suspicion that we have some kind of work to do to advance our collective evolution on this planet. This is it. We are the help! The clarion call has been issued. The world needs us now, as healers, teachers, spiritual activists, catalysts of change. There has never been a more critical time in the history of humanity. One could say that our very survival as a species is at stake here, and certainly, the quality of life on this planet.

There is no more time for hiding or playing small—for stuffing our essence, our hopes, and dreams deep inside in the questionable hope of avoiding conflict or rejection. It is time to stop running away, numbing out or self-medicating through drugs, alcohol, food, sex, TV, shopping, gaming, or social media. We can no longer afford to keep waiting for the cavalry or the ET intervention.

The time is now. Calling all heroes . . .

# CHAPTER 2
## WHY ME?

I am an unlikely candidate to be writing a book about power, heroism, and leadership. I am predominantly an introvert, and sharing my story here is a stretch for me. But I felt a strong pull to tell you more about me and what I've learned on my own heroic journey.

I chose several important personal stories to illustrate that shifting our relationship to power is not only doable, but accessible to anyone willing to embark on a journey of self-discovery, personal healing, and self-expression. I trust that some aspect of my experience, thoughts, or perceptions may inspire and support you in your own process of transformation, liberation, and empowerment. There is nothing more exciting, honorable, or heroic.

I was born in Cuba in 1959, the year of the Communist revolution, and lived there for ten years until my family came to the U.S. by way of Spain.

My early years in Cuba began to color the way I related to power and leadership. As in all totalitarian regimes, leadership was authoritative, top down. Power was imposed by force and through fear. The existing power structure was questioned at great risk.

In Cuba, as soon as one requested permission to emigrate, one was cast as a *gusano*, or worm. In primary (elementary) school, my older sister and I, who had been customarily at the top of the class, suddenly stopped receiving the "Vanguardia" award once it became known that our family had applied for an exit visa. At breaks we were not given milk and cookies along with the other kids. Some teachers singled us out in mean-spirited ways.

In totalitarian regimes the government has eyes everywhere; one must always be careful of what one says and to whom. In Cuba there was a "Defense Committee" in every block: a member of the Communist Party whose job was to keep an eye on the comings and goings of everyone on the block. Since my parents were involved in anti-revolutionary activities at the time, we grew up with the implicit message to stay close, not be seen, and not stand out. Fear ruled. It was not spoken about, but it was palpable. As kids we were protected and sheltered from most of it, but how could it not seep through when my parents' circle of friends kept diminishing as some went to prison, others, to the firing squad, and most left for exile? What do you say to kids when they see their mom distracting and delaying a scary-looking government official at the front door while their father hurls pounds and pounds of illegal black market beef over a wall into the neighbor's backyard?

Then there was the Church. Though in Communist Cuba the Church was sidelined, oppressed, and even persecuted at times, in my family it held even greater power than the state—the type of power one did not question: hierarchical, patriarchal, and very much externalized.

At least powerful women were not foreign to me. My older sister was a natural born leader, and my father's older sisters were also strong influences growing up. My teachers and principals were all women. I grew up accustomed to women in powerful roles. Even though ecclesiastic and governmental power structures were male-driven and Latin machismo was implicit and prevalent in the culture, at home my mother ruled the roost. My father, a psychiatrist, supported us in a multitude of ways: providing for his family; helping out with homework; and, in the absence of viable TV programming, tirelessly finding time to invent stories and create games for our entertainment and education. He was brought into family disciplinary affairs only in serious situations.

My mother, though a constant source of unconditional love, was the disciplinarian and master of "the look," which was enough to have us settle down. In our family, power was dispensed by Church, parents, and country, in that order.

I have always been an outsider. In Cuba, besides being called *gusano*, I was sometimes called "sissy" by other boys because I had female friends and felt more comfortable hanging out with them. I was a quiet, introverted, and bookish boy who did not enjoy fighting and rough play at breaks, and who never excelled at baseball—the national pastime—or other team sports. When we first came to the U.S. we lived in Milledgeville, a small town in central Georgia, where I stood out as a foreigner whose background and interests differed from those of my peers. In 8th grade I was enrolled in a private military academy, which I detested. I witnessed cruel abuses of power under the guise of teaching discipline and "toughening up" the young cadets.

After three years of a harsh rural Georgian exile and swim-or-sink initiation into life in America, I learned the language and finally started to fit in. That was when my father completed the requisite training for immigrant psychiatrists and our family moved to Miami. In a small, all-boys Catholic school whose students were 99 percent Cuban-American, once again I stood out because of my Southern twang! Further complicating my feelings of alienation was the fact that by my early teens I was already harboring a deep dark secret: I knew I was gay.

As a result of always being the outsider—the "other"—I became masterful at deflecting attention and receding into the background. I misunderstood, feared, and rejected roles of power or leadership.

At home, my older sister held the reins of power among the children, leading the tight knit and close-in-age brood of nine with authority. Among the neighborhood kids she was always the ringleader, that is, until puberty hit, and she sadly assumed a more traditional "ladylike" façade, denying her innate power (at least on the surface). Rooted in misunderstandings of power and gender roles, her self-imposed disempowerment is no doubt tragic. Yet what is even more lamentable is that this experience is not unique to my sister, but still far too common among women.

To say that I was painfully shy as a teenager would not even begin to capture my experience. I was generally OK one-on-one, but clammed up as soon as a third person was introduced to the mix. To this day I am most comfortable in solitude, especially in nature; that is where I best rejuvenate my energies. Group interactions, particularly those in superficial social settings, can be energetically taxing; I don't do chitchat well.

I received all A's throughout high school except for one B, subconsciously sabotaging the possibility of being class valedictorian because I dreaded speaking in public. No way could I speak in front of hundreds of people. Paradoxically, in my family the implicit message to hide and not stand out too much stood side by side with a drive to excel. This family dynamic created an interesting conflict, as I strived to both be seen and not seen, to both excel and disappear into the background. Such ambivalence did not contribute to a healthy relationship to power.

Needless to say, I felt very disempowered growing up. I was deeply conflicted about being gay; the struggle to reconcile my all-encompassing Catholic religion with my sexuality became a gnawing existential conflict. I lived in constant inner despair and turbulence; mine was a schizoid double life lacking wholeness, authenticity, and congruence. I was trying to be something I wasn't, to meet the expectations of society, culture, and religion, as well as my own misunderstanding and internalized projection of my parents' expectations of me: that I would be a priest or a doctor, that I would excel in school, that I would marry and carry on the family name, that I would excel yet not draw too much attention to myself. In short, it is fair to say that my adolescence was one long, drawn out depression.

My first experience of power and leadership occurred when I became editor of *Vincam*, the high school news magazine. During my sophomore year the magazine experienced a power struggle and eventual schism between two groups, which unexpectedly resulted in my emerging as assistant editor as a junior. Though

I was terrified of stepping into a position of leadership that would—horrors!—force me to lead staff meetings, my stint as editor-in-chief during my senior year actually turned out well. I was able to bring unity and inspire action, participation, collaboration, and excellence from members of both splinter groups and from a wide variety of students—from nerdy intellectuals to artistic eccentrics to popular jocks. That year *Vincam* was the best it had ever been, and I attribute that to my being able to pull different people together and evoke the best from each of them.

While that realization didn't come until years later, in retrospect, that is when I first exhibited leadership qualities. I knew I had pulled off something that made a difference. I had effectively evoked excellence and passion from my peers—in spite of my shyness, and still managing to avoid the limelight as much as possible. I was much prouder of that accomplishment than I was of my high grade point average. While studying and getting good grades came naturally to me, this was a real stretch. It took a great deal of effort, high energy and transcending my fears . . . and it paid off.

Years later, while living in an ashram, or spiritual community, I rose to leadership quickly, on the force of my conviction and sense of mission—the same thing that drove to me to later start a nonprofit, write a book, and become a spiritual activist, of sorts.

So here I am, writing a book on power, heroism, and leadership. How does this life experience qualify me to write about such things?

In every crisis or painful situation there is always a silver lining, if we will only look for it or allow it to reveal itself, and avoid falling into feelings of victimization: If it only hadn't been for *that*, then I would be happy or successful or _____ (fill in the blank). Because I had to struggle with existential questions at an early age, I became self-reflective and self-aware. I developed a deep sense of myself before my peers. I had to. For me, it was a question of survival. As a result, I often ended up playing the role of trusted counselor, mediator, peacekeeper. My own pain and alienation deepened my understanding of the human condition, enabling me to feel empathy and compassion for others.

It has been a long journey from self-hatred to self-acceptance. I now know who I am, and that's powerful. I am comfortable in my body, in my skin, at ease with my sensuality, sexuality—and spirituality. That's powerful too.

I live in a fairly constant state of gratitude—of grace. I am guided by a profound sense of purpose, a life of meaning, a sense of mission. My life is fully surrendered in service, and I've found a way to live in the presence of the sacred. I live a magical and miraculous life in which innumerable blessings are constantly showered upon me. I am surrounded by a loving and fiercely loyal family—in fact, two families, counting my former partner's family in California. Add to that a spiritual family of beloved sisters and brothers, all committed to their own process of transformation and to making a difference in this world. I stand free, without need of anyone's acceptance or validation. I have attained a level of freedom, choice, and nonattachment about relationships and sexuality. I am fortunate to frequently receive grateful feedback and acknowledgment from people in whose lives my work and presence have made a difference. I am fearless, meaning that I no longer allow fear to hold me back. I have peace of mind. I live in trust and in a symbiotic, connected, and integrated relationship with the universe, one from which we both grow and benefit and in which we delight.

All of that is so powerful, I can't help but marvel that this is my life!

Am I done? Of course not! In some ways, I've only just begun. But as it turns out, I do have something to say about power, leadership, and heroism. I hope and pray that my stories and insights bring you the same gifts I have enjoyed from doing this work.

# CHAPTER 3
## DESPERATELY SEEKING BALANCE

Although this book is clearly for anyone wishing to step more fully into an authentic expression of soulful power, it has a particular message for women. This stems from my conviction that the single most important thing that needs to happen in our world is the empowerment of women. The world is off balance when it comes to power between the genders—and that imbalance of power is at the root of most, if not all, of the problems we collectively face.

Overpopulation. Hunger. Poverty. Research indicates that if we want to change those conditions, we must begin by educating women. War? Because of their biologically deeper connection to life, women are generally much less inclined to destroy it.

The environment? How we treat our planet stems from a patriarchal fuck or kill, rape and pillage, extract and exploit mentality. With a sense of entitlement and little regard for sustainability or even survival, we take what we want from nature, consequences be damned.

WE SIMPLY CAN NO LONGER AFFORD A WHAM-BAM, THANK-YOU-MA'AM RELATIONSHIP TO THE EARTH!

The belief driving this book is that when women hold 50 percent of world leadership, all these issues will be addressed differently. Needless to say, not all women embody soulful power merely by virtue of their genitalia or X chromosome. To wit, Margaret Thatcher or Indira Gandhi. In our world today, a woman must feel as though she has to be extra tough to be seen and accepted as a credible leader. We do not need more of the arrogant, testosterone-fueled pseudo-power that leads to unilateral decisions, preemptive wars, an eye for an eye, you're either with us or against us, black-and-white thinking, and punitive policies!

While, undeniably, women have paid a steep price in terms of oppressive rules, abusive treatment, and lack of opportunity, the patriarchal system has also affected men negatively, hamstringing their authentic power and suppressing their full human potential. We will explore later ways of reimagining masculinity for 21st-century heroes.

In a sense, this book seeks to support the activation of the Sacred Feminine inside each one of us—regardless of our gender. The goal is not a return to matriarchy, but of a balance of power. And if we hope to find that balance in the world, it must begin within.

## SHE'S BAAACK!

While watching the film *Avatar* for the third time on IMAX 3D some years ago, I found myself pondering how interesting it was to find the audience rooting for the ETs when the choice was between life and death, between us and them. In other films such as *ET* and *Close Encounters* in which the ETs were also the good guys, such an existential choice was not present. But with *Avatar*, it turns out the enemy is *us*.

The 17th-century theologian François Fénelon said that all war was civil war. That was long before *Avatar* beautifully depicted the Gaia Theory—that of Earth as one sentient, interconnected organism. And long before scientists proved that all humans share 99.9 percent of our DNA. That development now means his centuries-old words can be taken quite literally. Despite such superficial differences as skin pigmentation—not to mention our beliefs—we are ONE race. Significantly, we also share 98.4 percent of our DNA with chimps, and 50 percent with bananas!

*Avatar* pits archetypal forces locked in mortal conflict: Nature/The Goddess (Eywa/Gaia) vs. the culmination of the patriarchy—the Military/Industrial Complex—personified by the Colonel and the Company Guy. We watch in helpless dismay as the Colonel contentedly admires the destruction that he has prematurely ordered at terrible cost to the indigenous Na'vi, so that he can get back to his compound in time for dinner.

A college friend, Michelle, had a gender theory about New York architecture: The Empire State? Feminine—tall slender, graceful elegant lines. The World Trade Center? Masculine—studly, angular lines. The Chrysler? An over-the-top, flamboyant drag queen. Is it not fascinating that it was the bastion of masculinity, the center for trade and commerce, that was attacked (along with the Pentagon—housing the most powerful military in world history) by an organization that was one of most oppressive of women in the world? In a way, the symbolism of 9/11 was the patriarchy imploding, taking itself out. The Goddess is back.

In *Avatar*, the ultimate source of power turns out to be the Goddess, the Great Mother. The Na'vi have no fancy weapons, but their connectedness to Nature unleashes her power. The Sacred Feminine emerges victorious: Intuition. Living in balance. The interconnectedness of all life. The ancient wisdom of the ancestors.

Among the Na'vi, leadership is shared by coequal leaders, mated for life. The female interprets the messages from Eywa and provides the all-important spiritual guidance. The Sacred Masculine and the Sacred Feminine have struck balance.

In his fascinating historical analysis, *The Alphabet Versus the Goddess*, best-selling author, inventor, and surgeon Leonard Shlain posits a theory that the patriarchy arose with the birth of the alphabet—at the very same point that the male, monotheistic deity first appears. Reading and writing trigger linear, abstract thinking and activate the left brain. The image, holistic thinking, the Goddess, and feminine values are oppressed whenever cultures achieve literacy.

Shlain connects the birth of the suffragist and modern women's rights movement with the discovery of photography and the typewriter—which involves both sides of the brain in the writing process—in the mid-1800s. Interestingly, *Avatar* triggers both left and right brains: In addition to visually stunning images, we must read subtitles to understand what the Na'vi are saying. Image and words. Balance. The movie is a wake-up call for each one of us to arise and help restore our planet before it is too late. Nothing is insurmountable when we come together as One.

Yes, we are the enemy. We are also the avatars.

## WHAT DOES A GAY MAN HAVE TO SAY TO WOMEN ABOUT POWER?

Author Judy Grahn theorizes that the way power shifted from matriarchy to patriarchy was through men who crossed sexual and gender boundaries, those we today refer to as gay, bisexual, transgender, or queer. These men were the only ones who had access to the sacred temples that were populated and run by women, and that contained the secrets of wisdom.

If so, as a gay man today I feel a personal responsibility to help shift back the balance of power—this time to a place of equality and equilibrium.

Furthermore, as I put forth in my first book, *Coming Out Spiritually*, in many settings throughout history, people we today refer to as lesbian, gay, bisexual, or transgender were not only spiritually inclined but were honored for the spiritual roles of service and leadership they provided. Because in many indigenous contexts we were thought to contain the essence of both male and female, one of the roles we played was mediating between the genders. It is with a deep sense of humility that I take on that same role now in this exploration on power, as well as that of spiritual activist, another role to which LGBTQ people have often gravitated.

## SO, ARE YOU IN?

Is your answer to the call for heroes a YES?

Excellent! Thank you! We sure can use you.

Now that you have accepted the call, I want to share a couple of details in preparation for the road ahead. There will be challenges and tasks, some offered as hero tasks—assignments throughout the book—and others that life will present. When we make a powerful declaration of intent to life, it has a way of testing our mettle and resolve. Don't despair. Stay on the path. You will be supported on the journey in magical and unexpected ways and the rewards are infinitely worth it!

One thing I have learned through facilitating countless retreats over the last three decades is that applying them to our lives is what makes these lessons stick. To support that process as we launch into our heroic journey, each chapter will have Power Practices—the hero tasks or missions to be completed (should you choose to accept them). These are designed to make the experience proactive and participatory. They will help you embody these concepts and integrate them into your daily life.

I recommend you create a journal just for this work. Read the questions and relax; get quiet so you can hear your true answers. Write them down and move on to the next chapter. When you work with the suggestions and questions in these books, the rewards will multiply, and you will begin to feel clearer and more empowered. You'll quickly begin seeing yourself from a more expanded perspective.

At the end of all my retreats we also talk about reentry, anticipating the effects that going back into our daily lives will have on our enhanced awareness. Life has a way of getting in the way of our new perspectives and choices. The next chapter presents a way of understanding how the mind works, also a critical aspect of my retreats. This understanding will support you to not get tricked by its limiting beliefs and boring behavior patterns. One thing that always comes up during the reentry discussion is the power of community in supporting ourselves and our new choices. We encourage participants to stay connected and reach out to each other for support when they start slipping into old patterns of self-doubt or unhealthy behavior.

Toward that end, please include yourself in our **Unleash Your Inner Hero Facebook Group**. Let's stay connected and support each other on our heroes' journey!

## POWER PRACTICES

- What does heroism mean to you? In your journal, capture some of your thoughts about what it means to be a hero. Have you ever secretly thought of yourself as heroic? Looking back at your life through the prism of everyday heroes we are exploring here, create a list of examples of situations or experiences where you are now able to see the heroism of your actions.

- On a "heroism scale" from 1 to 10, where would you place yourself today? Just a general feeling about where you are now is enough. At the end of the book I'll ask this question again.

- Who are your heroes? Begin by creating a list of heroes. Who has inspired you with the heroic nature evident in their lives? You can include famous people or those from your personal life. Harriet Tubman? Mother Theresa? Winston Churchill? Eleanor Roosevelt? Princess Diana? Greta Thunberg? Father Mychal Judge? Your father or mother, perhaps? A teacher?

- To mark the beginning of this journey, create your Hero Altar. First find a small table, fireplace mantel, or even a corner on your desk or dresser that you will designate as your altar. On it you might include photographs of your heroes identified above, illustrations, amulets, power stones or crystals to inspire you on the journey and serve as reminders of your commitment. The altar is intended to work as a reminder, to alter everyday perception beyond the ordinary and commonplace. You're walking around getting dressed or on the way to the kitchen to make coffee and the altar triggers an "Oh, that's right. I'm a freakin' hero on a hero's journey!" Please share a picture of your altar on the Facebook group.

# PART II

## THE EMPIRE OF THE EGO

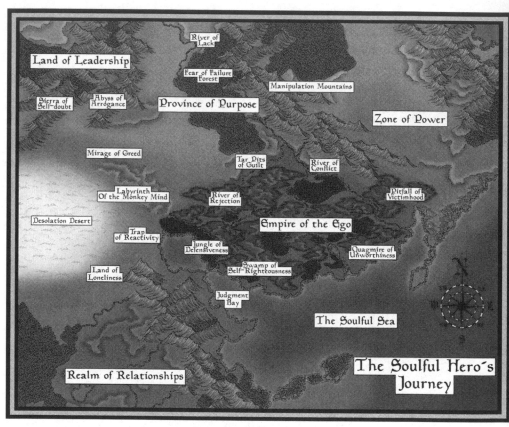

The following labels appear on the map:

Land of Leadership

River of Lack

Fear of Failure Forest

Manipulation Mountains

Sierra of Self-doubt

Abyss of Arrogance

Province of Purpose

Zone of Power

Mirage of Greed

Tar Pits of Guilt

River of Conflict

Labyrinth Of the Monkey Mind

River of Rejection

Pitfall of Victimhood

Desolation Desert

Empire of the Ego

Trap of Reactivity

Jungle of Defensiveness

Quagmire of Unworthiness

Land of Loneliness

Swamp of Self-Righteousness

Judgment Bay

The Soulful Sea

Realm of Relationships

The Soulful Hero's Journey

Map of the Soulful Hero's Journey

# CHAPTER 4
## THE HERO'S JOURNEY BEGINS

### LIFTING THE VEIL

We are living in apocalyptic times. What further evidence do we need than fire falling from the sky, raining unspeakable destruction on Iraq, Afghanistan, Syria, or Yemen? Worldwide plagues and pestilence, bleeding oceans, blackened waters, natural disasters and Earth changes, war and conflict and famine . . . we are witnessing it all.

Yet in ancient Greek the real meaning of *apocalypse* was not about the end of the world; the word meant "lifting the veil." In our times, veils are being lifted and all-powerful wizards are being revealed as simple, cowardly con men hiding behind a curtain. Examples today of veils being lifted include the corporate scandals, the church scandals, the banking-driven economic crisis, and the rise of populist movements—at both ends of the political spectrum—that challenge existing power structures.

In fact, veils are also being lifted about the nature of power itself.

> IN ANCIENT GREEK, THE REAL MEANING OF *APOCALYPSE* WAS "LIFTING THE VEIL."

At a time when the old, fear-based, command and control, patriarchal ways of doing things are being revealed as no longer sustainable, many of us are evaluating the impact of power on every area of our lives—interpersonal relationships, sex, work, politics,

27

religion and so on. As new and emerging energies for change become increasingly evident, what we need are new models that embody more-integrated expressions of power.

How can heroes relate to power in a different way that's not about hierarchy, fear, force, or abuse? How can we find a way without stepping on anyone, squelching them, putting them down in order to prop ourselves up and feel powerful?

In this first book of the *Calling All Heroes* series, *Awakening the Soul of Power*, we explore the difference between worldly power, or egoic power, and soulful or spiritual power.

So, what do I mean by "soulful" or "spiritual" power? First, we must differentiate the word *spiritual* from the word *religious*. The word *religion* comes from the Latin word *religare*, which means "to rebind." The word is laden with innumerable abuses of power and conflicting dogma throughout history and thus, to me, feels binding, restrictive.

I am not suggesting that religions do not serve a purpose or have not contributed to human evolution in positive ways. Of course, they have. But to the degree that they have set themselves up as necessary intermediaries to the sacred and externalized the divine, and to the degree that they fuel hatred, exclusiveness, and tribal consciousness, they have also done great harm.

In contrast, the word *spiritual* originates from the Latin *spirare,* which means both "breath" and "spirit" and is the root of the words *respiration, inspiration,* and *expiration.* The word for "spirit" and "breath" is the same in many spiritual traditions and languages. For me, that ineffable and undefinable force that animates us approximates what it means to be "spiritual." Similarly, the word *soul* refers to our essence, our own individual and very personal connection to the source of life that animates the Universe—and of which it is a unique expression.

## RING, RING . . . IT'S FOR YOU

In his seminal book, *The Hero with a Thousand Faces*, Joseph Campbell describes three basic phases of the mythological hero's journey. Found in ancient myths and in literature and films, the journey consists of three stages.

Phase 1: Call to adventure. The hero abandons the safety and comfort of the world she knows and embarks on an adventure into the unknown. Wonder Woman's perfect world on the Amazon island of Themyscira is shattered by the intrusion of pilot Steve Trevor and the Nazis trying to capture him, and she is thrust into a perilous adventure in a destructive world. In *The Lord of the Rings*, Frodo leaves his comfortable yet complacent and boring life in the Shire and follows Gandalf on a life-changing journey fraught with danger—and filled with meaning, connection, and purpose. Similarly, Neo chooses the red pill and leaves the illusory perfection of the Matrix in search of truth and freedom, no matter how harsh and risky.

Phase 2: Initiation. During this stage, the hero faces villains and overcomes trials and tribulations. On our heroic journey we face ourselves, our fears, our shadow, our inner demons. We are willing to look into what makes us tick and explore the difficult questions: Where do we sell out on our power? What effect did past and yet unhealed traumas have on our current behavior? What patterns do we see in our relationships? What kind of situations trigger us and result in interpersonal conflict? In this stage we encounter allies and come up against our adversaries—our personal villains.

Phase 3: Return. The hero survives the journey, having overcome all sorts of adversities or learned from his failures. Now transformed, she returns home filled with experience and wisdom, which she shares with the community. Dorothy bids goodbye to her friends in Oz, clicks her heels and transports herself home with a vastly expanded sense of herself and her capabilities, with a renewed and deepened appreciation of the meaning of home. In *The Lion King*, Simba faces himself, learns responsibility, discovers love, and returns to the pride to avenge his father and reclaim his throne.

On our own heroic journey, then, the first step is the call. We leave the safety of our comfort zone and embark on a journey within—the greatest adventure into what, for most of us, has been mostly uncharted territory.

That you picked up or were attracted to a book series entitled *Calling All Heroes* lets us know quite a bit. Maybe you are just receiving a call to adventure. *The* call. Something has not been working. Maybe life works well enough for you but deep down inside you feel as though there has to be more. Mediocrity and complacency are eating you up inside. You know you have more to offer; something inside you longs for expression. Maybe the call came through a life crisis: A relationship just crashed big time, or you got fired from a job. Or possibly you just returned home from a heroic adventure and are ready for a deeper understanding and integration of the process you just experienced.

Whatever the case may be, you have said YES to the call for heroes. The Map of the Soulful Hero's Journey at the beginning of this chapter illustrates an overview of the journey we will take on this path, depicting the different territories we will visit. On the road to freedom and personal empowerment, the first destination is the Empire of the Ego.

As we launch into this journey of transformation, it is important to clarify that the ego we discuss here is not the one from psychological models of personality such as Freud's id, ego, and superego. Nor are we talking about the simple concept of having a "big ego," meaning arrogance or an inflated sense of self. It is that, to be sure, but it is so much more than that. The psychospiritual construct of the ego presented here is derived from spiritual teachings from the East.

We'll start by delving into how the ego—the villainous Warden of the Empire—keeps us from living into our power, and how we can escape its hold on our lives. When we do, we'll break free from its prison of fear, self-doubt, and limitation. We'll begin to enjoy a life of freedom and an expanded sense of who we are.

## KNOW THE VILLAIN IF YOU WANT TO BE FREE

Among the different types of retreats I offer, some have to do with relationships, others with personal empowerment, women's empowerment, life purpose, or leadership. Regardless of the theme, there are always two constants. One is breathwork, because in thirty years of being actively involved in spiritual and transformation circles all over the world, I have yet to come across anything that heals as deeply and as quickly as this extraordinary practice does. The other is teaching about the ego.

No matter what obstacles we have allowed to hold us back— whether keeping us playing small and not stepping fully into our power or our purpose, or keeping us from having relationships that are a match and that actually work—it all comes down to the ego. This aspect of our minds is the source of all our conflicts and discord in relationships. It is the reason for divorce and for war, the impediment to our happiness and fulfillment. It is the cause of suffering. And it is what keeps us from being our heroic selves, from living as heroes.

The ego is the Villain, our nemesis on our heroic journey. Heroes are selfless and sometimes sacrifice their life for the sake of others or for a cause; the ego is selfish and puts its needs ahead of everything else. Whereas heroes tend to be humble, the ego is arrogant, self-absorbed, and self-important. Heroes act in spite of their doubts, sometimes against impossible odds, risking failure, in the process transcending themselves (their egos) and any perceived limitations. The ego is complacent, lazy, entitled, and looks for the easy way out. It avoids responsibility and is often incapacitated by fear of failure. Alternatively, it can also reveal itself as obsessively driven to perfectionism, relentlessly attempting to prove its worth and to compensate for perceived inadequacies by holding itself and others to impossible standards.

The ego is that part of us that is always making comparisons, judging ourselves and others harshly. Stuck in feelings of anger, blame, and resentment, it lives in the realms of fear, shame, and guilt. It is possessive, calculating, and greedy. Ironically, as superior as it can tend to feel on the surface, it feeds on the approval of others and depends on external validation. While a hero is responsible and assumes ultimate accountability for all his actions, the ego is trapped in victim mode, blaming others and circumstances for its state of being.

## YOU ARE WHO YOU THINK YOU ARE

Experts theorize about a time when humans did not have an ego—a sense of individual identity—when we lived in a state of oneness with nature and the universe in a veritable Garden of Eden. Ken Wilber proposes that the birth of the ego was actually the first split in our consciousness, the "fall from grace" that was then mythologized in various cultures as the "expulsion from the garden."[1]

What was evolutionary and revolutionary about the ego's development then, is that it gave us a separate sense of self. *Ego*, in Latin, means "I." It sounds like this: "I am Christian, separate from Tom, Tina, or Teresa. This is who I am over here, distinct from you over there." This was a huge leap in evolution and has accounted for much of humanity's success—and many, if not most, of our failures.

*EGO*, IN LATIN, MEANS "I."

The ego serves as a unifying principle, a fulcrum of consciousness that makes sense of sensory information and past experience, even projecting into future possibilities and weaving all of that into a coherent sense of self. *Homo sapiens sapiens* can be interpreted to mean "humans who know that we know." We have the ability to reflect upon ourselves. Having a sense of self makes self-reflection possible, and that is part of the reason we have been so successful as a species.

As much of an evolutionary leap that the development of the ego was, we need to be conscious that it is also the reason for our present troubles: One price we paid for having a separate sense of self is that we lost awareness of our connection to the Universe. Because of that, we treat ourselves, each other, and the planet without respect or even regard to our own survival. To be sure, having awareness of time and being able to project into the future is a great skill to have, but one that also comes with its own set of drawbacks, including a sense of our own mortality.

A strong ego also means that threats to our fragile, artificial, and false sense of self trigger the same response in the body as if our physical survival were at stake. In other words, our brain biochemistry responds to perceived psychological threats in the same way as if we were about to be chased by a saber-toothed tiger. In the latter situation it's beneficial to have our muscles tense up, our heart rate increase and blood pressure rise as our bodies get ready to spring into action. It's a matter of survival. But living at DEFCON 1—in maximum readiness defense mode against anticipated attacks—becomes counterproductive and even harmful, especially in situations in which only our psychological and emotional self (our ego) is at risk. That is one reason we live with such high and constant levels of worry and stress. The body can only take so much of that before the effects start impacting our health, physically and emotionally. The result? Cancer, heart attacks, ulcers, depression, anxiety.

As Peter Russell writes, "Fear also leads to worry. We worry about what others might be thinking of us. We worry about what we have done or not done, and about what might or might not happen to us. When we worry like this, our attention is caught up in the past or the future. It is not experiencing the present moment. Perhaps the saddest irony of all is that this worry prevents us from finding that which we are really seeking. The goal of every person is, in the final analysis, a comfortable state of mind. Quite naturally, we want to avoid pain and suffering, and feel more at peace. But a mind that is busy worrying cannot be a mind that is at peace. Other animals do not experience . . . all the worries that come from having a vulnerable sense of self. They are probably at peace much more of the time. Human beings may have made a great leap forward in consciousness, but at our present stage of development we are no happier for it—quite the opposite."[2]

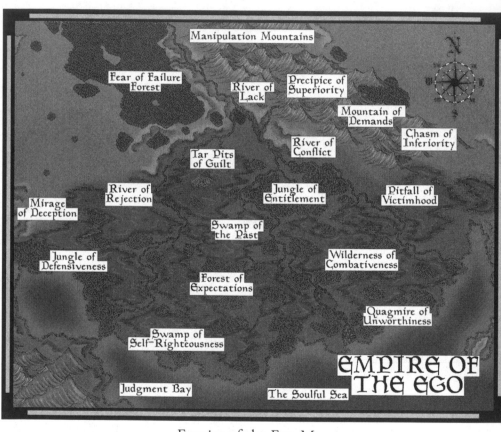

Empire of the Ego Map

# CHAPTER 5
## WHO ARE YOU, REALLY?
## PROFILING THE EGO

So how does the ego work?

The model of the ego presented here evolved from one created by my former teacher, IsanaMada, later known as Maia Dhyan. Unfortunately, her book, *A Call to Greatness,* is out of print. My portrayal of the model will in some key ways mirror its source, as it was passed down to me in the oral tradition, having witnessed her teach it on numerous occasions and then having been trained by her to present it in seminars, which I have been doing now for thirty years. I also assisted her in writing that book.

The present model includes my own additions and adaptations developed over many years of radical self-observation and working with people privately and in retreat settings.

The ego is sometimes referred to as the "diminished self," meaning that it is a small part of who we are. Spiritual teachers occasionally use the metaphor of a stadium to illustrate this: if we placed a baseball in the center of the field, that would be the ego. Who we are is actually the stadium.

Problems arise because that tiny part of us has gotten confused and believes that it is all of who we are. It has, for the most part, hijacked our lives. We have allowed it to run the show for too long. Tragically, we sell ourselves short, play small and make critical choices about our lives from the extremely limited and fear-based perspective of our egos.

As *A Course in Miracles* explains,

"This fragment of your mind is such a tiny part of it, that, could you but appreciate the whole, you would see instantly that it is like the smallest sunbeam is to the sun. Or like the faintest ripple on the surface of the ocean. In its amazing arrogance, this tiny sunbeam has decided it is the sun; this almost imperceptible ripple hails itself as the ocean. Think how alone and frightened is this little thought, this infinitesimal illusion, holding itself apart, against the universe.... Do not accept this little, fenced-off aspect as your Self. The sun and ocean are as nothing, beside what you are. The sunbeam sparkles only in the sunlight, and the ripple dances as it rests upon the ocean. Yet in neither sun nor ocean is the power that rests in you."[3]

As with any model, the one presented in these pages is not perfect, yet it provides a useful and simple way to understand the ego and how it works. When I first encountered these teachings, I realized they were exactly what I had been looking for when I went into psychology—something that would help me understand how my mind works; why I did the things I did; why I sometimes seemed to sabotage my goals, needs, and desires; why I got caught in repetitive and fruitless behavior ruts; why happiness eluded me. How I wish I would have learned this earlier from my psychiatrist father or my psychology teachers in college! If we were taught this at a much earlier age, life would be so much easier to navigate and our world a much better place in which to live.

The Ego Model

## EGOLLUM

In *The Lord of the Rings*, Gollum is a ghost of what he used to be, a shadow of his authentic self. Once a hobbit, he was corrupted and deformed by the powerful magic of the ring he found. He is deceptive, manipulative and, when pushed, outright dangerous. He is greedy, entitled, and obsessed with his "precious" ring to the degree that nothing else matters.

The ego is envisioned here as a Gollum-esque figure, a hybrid between Gollum and a multihanded Hindu deity. Gollum is inauthentic—a dangerous fake—acting in a subservient manner until an opportunity presents itself and then becoming aggressive, vengeful, and treacherous. Our ego is likewise devious, cunning, insidious, and untrustworthy. With its sharp, pointy teeth the ego has quite a bite when it feels crossed or slighted, or if it doesn't get what it wants. The ego can be slick, charming, disarming, and seductive. Its manipulation strategies include guilt, sabotage, and passive-aggressiveness.

It waits and pounces at the right opportunity, sometimes pitifully and halfheartedly, almost in vain; at other times, the ego comes with a knife in its teeth, leaving a bloody trail in its wake. Because of that we have to keep a constant and mindful eye on our ego. We can't get complacent and turn our back on it.

The ego takes everything personally as an affront to its very identity, its core sense of worth, and then works even harder to defend against the affront. When it feels mistreated or attacked, it holds on to its perception of having been wronged or victimized and waits for an opportunity to get revenge, or to prove that it's right. The ego is petty and sulks when it doesn't get its way, stewing in its mantra of "Poor me" and in its juices of discontent.

## The Greedy, Grabby, Control-Freak Monkey Mind

Like Gollum, the ego is self-absorbed, selfish, and entitled. It lives by the motto "It's mine." It wants what it wants, and it wants it now! With one hand it grasps and attempts to hold on to things and people, whatever it can grab. It is needy, bratty, clingy, and possessive. When I teach the ego to younger folk, I refer to it as the Inner Brat and, to illustrate, use the scene of the seagulls on the fishing pier in *Finding Nemo*: "Mine . . . mine . . . mine . . ."

Because it is stuck in beliefs of lack and insufficiency, the ego hoards things. In relationships with others it is needy and tries to hold on to people. This belief that there is not enough is at the source of its fierce competitiveness. With that same grasping hand, the ego reaches into the world and tries to control people and circumstances. The ego is a major control freak! Its attempts to micromanage life and control all possible outcomes are futile.

They would be laughable if the effort did not cause so much stress and unhappiness.

The ego's goal is to maintain the status quo and keep things exactly as they are. As a result, it resists change, even if change is from, at best, a comfortable situation to, at worst, a miserable one. It does not distinguish between them. That means that anything that signifies change will be threatening to the ego, which will resist the change and come up with all sorts of self-defeating reasons and self-sabotaging strategies to avoid it, such as putting off getting back to the gym or changing unhealthy eating habits; signing up and then rescheduling that workshop, retreat or counseling session; canceling a date or showing up late for a job interview.

In the model, the ego is featured with narrow slits for eyes, indicating that it has a hard time seeing what's right in front of it. With the mirror it holds in one hand, it sees clearly into the past and vividly remembers past hurts and betrayals, which it holds on to. The mirror is also about looking good, since the ego, by definition, is narcissistic.

Similarly, the tiny ears refer to its impaired hearing; the ego has a challenging time hearing the truth in the present. It spends most of the time rehashing and ruminating about a past that is gone and will never happen again, or fantasizing, projecting, and hallucinating about a future that may—or may not—come to be.

If all that was not bad enough, it has a huge mouth that is constantly chattering. The ego has very strong opinions and something to say about everyone and everything, exhausting itself with its endless monologue and relentless machinations.

It is what the Buddhists refer to as the "monkey mind." All day long our minds jump from thought to thought in the same way a monkey swings from one branch to the next, sounding something like this:

> I'm walking down the street and see a woman wearing a T-shirt with a palm tree, which reminds me that I forgot to call the gardener for the dinner party I'm throwing next week . . .

which then reminds me that I haven't called my friend Luna to invite her because I've been going nonstop and I forgot to mention it when we were having lunch last week . . . which, hmmm, now that I think of it, I'm getting kinda hungry now and maybe I should eat something . . . and there's that new Mexican restaurant that opened up downtown, right across the street from the bank and . . . come to think of it, that's a great idea because I have to make a deposit . . . and since I'll be out and about, I might as well go and pick up those shirts that have been at the dry cleaners for three months now . . .

And on and on it goes. Yikes! In a matter of seconds, I am now about 15 thoughts removed from the palm tree T-shirt. That's what goes on inside our heads all day long, from the minute we get up in the morning, before our feet have even hit the floor, to the moment when we fall asleep at the end of the day—that is, assuming we are able to, because often monkey mind keeps us awake well into the night with its endless chatter. Sadly, most of the time the chatter is less than kind and compassionate. The ego can be quite cruel, especially to ourselves.

## Do You Really Still Need That Armor?

The ego has surrounded and encased itself in layers of armor that have taken years to develop, like scar tissue that keeps getting thicker as it gets reinjured. With its forearm bracers as shields, it walks around in a perpetual state of defensiveness, anticipating and warding off perceived wrongs and attacks, sometimes striking the first blow preemptively, just in case.

The ego believes that this attitude of defensiveness keeps it safe; its constant state of attack readiness gives it the illusion of power. It regards emotions and vulnerability as weakness. Yet, as the ego walks around all stressed out and fearful, with crossed arms ready to ward off perceived attacks, it effectively keeps itself behind the bars of its own self-made prison. Though defensiveness may have served a valid purpose at some point in our lives, now it's counterproductive; it fends off the possibility of deep connection and creates discord in our relationships. The ego has not learned, as we will see later, that vulnerability is a more powerful and liberating way of being. Heroes have learned that, counterintuitively, the real power is in vulnerability, in defenselessness.

The truth is that underneath the ego's defensiveness is fear. Beneath its bravado, façades and braggadocio, the ego is a prisoner of its own fear and insecurities. It behaves in certain ways or avoids actions, people, and situations in reaction to or overcompensating for that.

## POWER PRACTICES

- Think of a recent time when someone in your life took personally something you said or did that wasn't intended that way. It didn't have to be perceived that way. Give examples and capture in your journal.

- How about a recent time your ego took something personally? How else might have you looked at or responded to the situation?

- What is a recent example of someone in your life resisting change or being a control freak? What about a recent example where you behaved in those ways? Record details and any insights in your journal.

- What is a recent example of someone in your life being defensive in a conversation? What about a recent example where you behaved in that way? Record details and any insights in your journal.

Victim
Self-Hatred
Doormat
Undeserving

Combative
Self-Important
Arrogant
Entitled

The Extreme Seesaw

# CHAPTER 6
## YO, WANNA RETHINK THAT STRATEGY?

The ego has an agenda to win. In all human interactions, it wants to win at all costs. If it can't win, it wants to be right. When the ego can't be right, it wants to save face, to look good; if it can't do that, it will do anything to survive.[4] We are talking about psychological survival, although to the ego, losing an argument or being wrong feels terminal.

### YOU REALLY WANT TO PLAY ON THE EXTREME SEESAW?

The ego's experience is one of extremes. It either feels superior to others (Who do they think they are treating me this way?") or inferior ("I can't believe I did it again; there is something seriously wrong with me!"). It goes up and down all day from one extreme to the other as if on a seesaw, fluctuating from feeling combative and walking around with a huge chip on its shoulder ("Don't even think about getting in my way!") to victim ("I have the worst luck. Everything always happens to me. Poor me!").

The tragic part of the Extreme Seesaw is that we find ourselves in the power of other people and prey to life's circumstances. We might get up in the morning feeling at the top of the world, take a nice, warm shower, put on our favorite shirt, and enjoy a delicious breakfast. The weather is gorgeous as we drive ourselves to work, singing along to our favorite playlist with careless abandon. Yet, when we get to the office, a co-worker says something to us the wrong way and that's it. We are off and running, either exploding into superior/combative mode, whether we think or speak it. ("How dare you treat me this way?") or plummeting into inferior/victim ("I really messed that one up! I knew things were going too well; I've been waiting for the other shoe to drop.") This is a sad way to live. We find ourselves at the mercy of other egos that have even less of a clue and whose lives are often even more messed up than ours, and to situations over which we have no control. Talk about giving away our power—power over our emotional state, our overall sense of well-being, the quality of our day and our experience of life!

## He Ain't Heavy; He's My Past

The model depicts the wounded ego, the unhealed ego. It has survived quite a number of battles and skirmishes and has accumulated the evidence to prove it, as shown by the Band-Aid, bruises, and scars. These "buttons" portray old wounds such as separation, alienation, abandonment, and betrayal; they represent the belief that there is something wrong with us, that we are unworthy or damaged goods.

The Bag of Past

With another hand the ego holds a bag filled with the past. Trouble is, we never know what aspect of its past baggage will be triggered in the present, which one of those unhealed bruises is going to be resurrected, causing a reaction in the present to a previously similar situation that took place in the past. What a tragic way to live, controlled by others, our pasts, our unresolved issues! Someone figures out one of our buttons and presses it, causing an immediate reaction in the present, as we hit back and splatter them against the wall. What we are actually reacting to is a previous similar situation from our pasts, or an accumulation of instances in which we stuffed and suppressed ourselves, unable to speak our truth or take a stand for ourselves.

## POWER PRACTICE

- Can you identify some of your more prominent buttons? Think about what has caused you trouble in the past. What kind of behaviors or situations upset you or get you all worked up? For example, are they situations where you feel treated unfairly or perhaps unseen, unvalued, or unappreciated? Is it when others cheat or lie or perhaps when they show up late or don't do what they said they would do? Write in your journal as reactions in the present surface. What patterns do you begin to see? In what type of situations do you feel more threatened or insecure? Work? Romantic? Family?

## KARMA CHAMELEON

In *The Billboard Book of #1 Hits,* Boy George explains to author Fred Bronson, "The song ("Karma Chameleon") is about the terrible fear of alienation that people have, the fear of standing up for one thing. It's about trying to suck up to everybody. Basically, if you aren't true, if you don't act like you feel, then you get Karma-justice, that's nature's way of paying you back."[5]

The Mask

The ego is a master of disguise. With its collection of theatrical masks, it is quick to stifle and cover up its emotions and put on a façade. It changes itself to fit into different situations, to blend in and not make waves. The ego fears rejection and abandonment, and will cloak itself, sell itself short, and do just about anything to avoid being left alone. It adapts to its own filtered interpretation of the expectations of family, others, and the society in which it lives. Keeping a lid on its authentic feelings, emotions, and preferences, the ego discloses only a caricature of itself to the world, hoping desperately for acceptance. Or, alternatively, it is quick to dramatize a situation or condition to elicit sympathy or manipulate a desired outcome. The irony is, of course, that with all its inauthentic shenanigans and protective armor, too often the ego accomplishes the very thing it is trying to avoid. It effectively drives people away or continues to feel unseen, separate and disconnected, fearing rejection and abandonment. The strategy is doomed to fail. Abort mission.

## POWER PRACTICES

- What masks do you still use? How do you hide your true self at home, work, or social outings?

- Which type of situations are likely to trigger an inauthentic response in you? Is it, for example, when there is a risk of rejection or being judged? Does it tend to happen in social or professional situations?

- Can you identify an underlying fear? What are you trying to cover up or protect? What might happen if people were able to see the real you?

# CHAPTER 7
## WEAPONS OF HAPPINESS DESTRUCTION

As we saw above, part of the ego's agenda is being right. The Trap of Being Right is such a strong lure for humans that we have been known to give up our body, even our life, rather than give up this stance.

This dynamic is particularly challenging for those of us who suffer the curse of always being right. Well, almost always. The bottom line truth is that even when we are (usually) right, so what? As they say in spiritual circles: "Would you rather be right or happy?" (I feel you! Of course, that's the perfect way to load the dishwasher!)

We can too easily fall into the trap—a subtly self-righteous, arrogant way of being—that closes the heart and causes harm to our relationships. That last smug "told ya!" may have felt good in the moment, but was it worth it? How does it feel on the receiving end? In relationships, being right is an occupational hazard. The Trap of Being Right has snared many a worthy hero and resulted in innumerable—and unnecessary—power struggles.

Simply introducing a healthy "maybe" softens the hard edge of the ego's self-righteousness. Rather than assuming that we know why someone else did that was wrong or ascribing meaning to their actions, we extend the benefit of the doubt. We walk even for a moment in their shoes.

Needless to say, this does not mean that we cannot have strong convictions or take a stand for issues we believe are right. After all, we are talking about personal empowerment and living heroic lives! Rather, it addresses the self-righteous attitude of the ego, which is a source of conflict in our relationships. It is not so much being right or wrong but the *need* to be right that gets us into trouble. Being right may bring about a sense of immediate satisfaction, even validation, but impede a long-lasting and peaceful sense of well-being. This attitude of self-righteousness infects our relationships and causes others to shut down. It engenders resentment, defensiveness, and feelings of failure; it brings about separation and discord and puts a stop to dialogue and communication. At the same time, needing to be right gives other egos—that don't even know they are egos—something to buck up and defend against. Have you ever noticed what happens when someone is arguing to prove how right they are? Our ego gets ruffled and—whether internally or externally—argue back, trying hard to disprove them.

The ego's strong need to be right foments wars—both interpersonal and international. An argument can begin as a power struggle between two egos both trying to be right and wrestling for control. I push your button and then you push one of mine. Back and forth, this keeps escalating until one of us loses control and explodes, potentially bringing harm to the relationship. On a global scale, when this goes on long enough, we end up with the Middle East.

Consider the famous feud in American history between the Hatfields and the McCoys. After years of feuding and multiple people dead, the case had to go to the U.S. Supreme Court because, as it turned out, the dividing line between their properties was also the border between Kentucky and West Virginia, which involved issues of illegal extradition. Though the feud fermented in post-Civil War differences, property rights and romantic entanglements gone awry, it started over an argument about who owned a pig. Someone got stabbed and shot and a long cycle of revenge ensued.

Why is it that the ego hates being wrong? Likely, it confuses being right with being in a position of power and perceives being wrong as powerlessness. It identifies being wrong with failure, shame, inadequacy, mockery. Therefore, a simple disagreement can morph into a personal challenge, an affront to its sense of well-being and self-worth.

Self-righteousness thus masks a deeper fear than simply being wrong. Underlying the aversion to being wrong is likely a subconscious threat to self at the level of ego identity. To the ego, being right has become a means of self-validation: I am right; therefore, I am worthy. It has become an issue of survival.

Choose right or choose happy.

## POWER PRACTICES

- The more secure we are in ourselves, the less need we have to be right. When we feel that reactive, defensive need to be right rearing up its ugly little head, we can pause, take a couple of deep breaths and ask ourselves:

  - "What would it mean about me if I were in fact wrong?

  - What am I perhaps compensating for?

  - What will I lose in the (highly unlikely but all right, possible) event that I am wrong?"

- We can practice softening the stance of being right and we extend the benefit of doubt. "Maybe, just maybe, they are right and I am wrong. And you know what? I would be OK with that. My identity and sense of self are not tied into the need to be right. Being wrong about something does not take away my intelligence or my value. What is there to protect anyway?"

The Double-Edged Knife of Judgment

## TAMING THE BEAST IN YOUR HEAD

By now you can see the ego is your harsh inner critic—the intransigent, implacable, self-righteous, and just plain nasty judge inside your head. It's the voice that second guesses, the voice of self-doubt.

Among the ego's arsenal of weapons of happiness destruction (WHDs), we find the double-edged knife of judgment. Its hands are always ready to point the finger in blame. In its arrogance and self-importance, the ego appoints itself judge, jury, and prosecutor, all wrapped up into one. In its self-righteousness it knows, without any doubt, that whatever the guilty party did was absolutely wrong and what the punishment should be. It even doles out the punishment.

As the double-edged knife illustrates, we need to realize when we are judging others, we are judging ourselves to that same degree. Often, we do quite a number on ourselves, and are more cruel to ourselves than most anyone else could be!

For that reason, if nothing else, we need to begin to soften the hard edges of our ego's self-righteousness. How? We can consciously take on the practice of undermining its need to be right and extending the benefit of the doubt. (Later on, hopefully we can even extend some compassion.)

When the ego judges someone, it diminishes them and makes itself superior. This often takes the form of reaction formation, one the classic psychological defense mechanisms. This subconscious strategy plays out by dealing with certain suppressed beliefs by morphing them into their opposite. I often see this at retreats when participants have some variety of the "I'm not good enough" belief going on. Other versions might feel more like "I'm not worthy of love," "There is something wrong with me" or, more specifically, "I'm stupid," "I'm good for nothing" or "I'm too much this, not enough that." And yet, because believing that we are not good enough would be too hurtful and distressing, we often hide those feelings away in the closet of the subconscious and take on the opposite belief. So, scratch underneath arrogance and, more than likely, you will discover someone who is compensating for perceived feelings of inadequacy. If I am "superior" to others, then I can't be less than they are.

Incidentally, as we will see later, breathwork heals and dissolves those old beliefs at their core. Ultimately, they have no basis in reality. They are simply misunderstandings of young minds that did not know any better.

## POWER PRACTICES

- When you catch your inner judge in the act, the first thing to do is begin to disidentify with him. Name it: "There goes my ego, judging away!" Next, put yourself in the other person's shoes and begin to soften the ego's harsh, sense of separation, superiority, and self-righteousness, which says "I would never do that!" Simply tell yourself: "I too have been that way," and list some ways in which you have done that in the past. At the very least tell yourself "Perhaps, had I been born in their place, into their family situation and the culture and conditions in which they were raised, maybe I too could have been that way."

- What is your variety of "I'm not good enough," even if it's no longer active? (List possibilities.) What is your earliest memory of feeling that way?

## YOU BE YOU. I BE ME

The ego has an attitude of entitlement. It has **expectations** about how others should behave and demands about what it deserves and the way it should be treated. It has strong opinions about everything: how others should be, feel, think; what they should eat; what they should study; what they should do with their lives; who they should be with; how they should wear their hair and on and on. The outcome of that scenario is inevitable: disappointment on one end and resentment on the other.

Countless people are being dragged down and swallowed up by the quicksand of other people's expectations. How many lives are being lived half-assed? How many people are playing small, suppressing their potential, or giving up their dreams, just to conform with the expectations of others? How many relationships are being consumed by the inevitable resentment that sparks up?

The ego becomes upset or angry when another person is not what it thinks they should be, or when things don't happen quickly enough. Expectations lead to suffering and disappointment. But that sting of disappointment offers a clue—that our ego has been expecting people or things to turn out a certain way—and we can use that pain as a catalyst to change.

Freeing ourselves from the expectations and demands of others is so important—as is freeing them from ours. We allow others to be who they are, rather than trying to define, limit or pigeonhole who they should be. Because this includes our most significant and emotionally invested relationships—our family, our lovers, our partners—it's not easy. In fact, it's nothing less than heroic.

Ego expectations on steroids become **demands**. The ego issues ultimatums, whether spoken or not. "That's it! I'm outta here." Once we are conscious of its demands, however, we learn to accept reality as it is. This does not mean we don't encourage others to improve themselves or work towards change in the world. Heroes are not passive or fatalistic. It means that we learn to identify when we are coming from a place of ego. It means that we no longer allow it to run amok with its expectations and demands. It means that we manage or let go altogether of our own perceptions, preferences, or agendas that we try to impose on others. Because of the ego's micromanaging tendencies, at first this feels next to impossible. However, we learn to take a deep breath and allow others to make their own choices and mistakes, even when we feel certain of the outcome. Eventually it becomes easier as we realize that managing our own lives is a full-time job and we are not responsible for anyone else's. We embrace the fact that we all learn and grow through our mistakes.

We learn to act, while letting go of attachment to outcome. We let go of our desire for recognition or acknowledgment. We do good because it is in us to do so, because it gives us joy and satisfaction and a sense of meaning and purpose, not because we need praise or reward. The ego defines itself by externals: possessions, rank, education, or the recognition, adulation—or criticism—of others. We know how fickle all that is and what a recipe for disappointment it is to define oneself by extraneous factors.

This is not to say we should have no preferences or dreams or that we should not plan for our best possible outcome. We expect miracles but are not disappointed when they don't occur on our timeframe. We let go of the attachment to things turning out a certain way.

And needless to say, this does not mean we have to put up with behavior that does not work for us or situations or relationships that are not a match. But we approach those from a place that is not the limited perspective of the ego and its unexamined expectations. Instead, we stop and ask: Why do I want what I want? Have I taken on the views of society or family? Am I doing stuff just because that's the way it's always been done, the way my parents did it and their parents before them? At a recent retreat Ronaldo became aware of a pattern that had for years been a source of conflict. He realized that his harsh attitude toward his son's lackadaisical relationship to homework—over which they often locked horns even though the son performed acceptably academically—stemmed from a comment his own father had made to him as a child. He recalled being punished for not doing his homework and being told that to be a man and succeed in life he had to learn to complete all his responsibilities before even thinking about playing.

As we explore more deeply in Book 2, *Attracting and Nurturing Relationships That Work*, we learn what is and what is not negotiable for us, knowing that those may change as we grow and evolve.

## POWER PRACTICES

To help liberate your inner hero, take on this practice:

- Today, focus on noticing your expectations. That requires becoming more mindful of your thoughts. Set your timer for 30-minute intervals. When it goes off, notice what you're thinking about and capture the thought in your journal. When you notice an expectation, observe it. No need to judge or punish yourself. Notice it and choose otherwise. Let it go. Expectations may be subtle. You might notice yourself, for example, wishing that a co-worker would not laugh so loudly. Perhaps you notice your mood and outlook changing because your date from last night hasn't called or texted and it's already 11 am. Or you find yourself getting fidgety and upset at the slow teller trainee because the line at the bank is longer than you had planned for and your lunch break is coming to an end. Whatever it is, you can simply observe your expectations.

- If you're ready, you can go deeper and explore your role in the situation. For example, in the example above, did you allow enough time? What could you have done to leave a few minutes earlier? Contemplate what choices are available to you now. Act accordingly and free yourself from feeling trapped or victimized by a situation. You can also free yourself by simply noticing the expectations, letting them go, and simply accepting what is.

# Chapter 8
## Evolving Out of the Pitfall of Victimhood

The ego is stuck in victim mode. Another of the mantras it lives by is "Poor me. Woe is me." Common victim thought patterns include: "I got dealt a crappy hand in life." "If X situation had not happened or if Y condition were different, then everything would be fine." "If it weren't for the (fill-in-the-blank: sexism, racism, homophobia . . .) running rampant in society, then my life would be different, and I would be happy." "What can you do? It's a dog-eat-dog world."

This passive mindset and approach to life dwells in guilt and leads to pessimism, fatalism, helplessness, and hopelessness.

Though it can be subtle, the ego gets a payoff for being a victim. We will dive into this aspect more in depth later, but for now, just realize that if we are talking about being heroic and exploring paths to personal empowerment, there is no way around having to let go of the victim. On the journey to freedom this is unavoidable—and a small price to pay. As long as we are blaming someone or holding some external condition responsible for our state of being, we keep ourselves stuck and disempowered.

The Pitfall of Victimhood is, arguably, the trickiest trap to navigate in the Empire of the Ego. It's what most people struggle with at my retreats because it's a level of consciousness we are trying to transcend. Because the ego's strategies can be surreptitious and hard to spot, tearing up the victim card and refusing to use it as a power play is an act of personal liberation, empowerment, and heroism.

## POWER PRACTICE

- Did someone say or do something, and now you feel insecure, angry, or betrayed? Resist the tendency to make the situation or even the person wrong. Ultimately, it's not about them. No one can make you feel anything if you don't allow it, or if those feelings aren't already inside you. Instead, try to accept that you are in the situation and choose to use it as an opportunity for learning and for growth. Take time to be by yourself, maybe go for a walk and ask yourself: What is my role in it? What is my payoff? What am I feeling? When else have I felt this way? Keep going back in time as far as possible. When was the earliest time you remember feeling that way? Write down your insights or journal about the experience.

## TURNING THE MIRROR AROUND

Projection is another one of the classical defense mechanisms in psychology. It is triggered when some aspect of ourselves is too unacceptable for us to even look at, so we deny or reject that part and stash it away in the "shadow" of our subconscious. We then assign these undesirable feelings to someone else, projecting them out like a movie onto a screen: we are able to see clearly over "there" what we are blind to over "here."

Examples of this include self-righteous, judgmental, homophobic religious and political leaders—Ted Haggard, George Rekers, Larry Craig, Mark Foley, and Eddie Long, to name a few. How often do we hear about these types getting busted in sex scandals with rent boys or male congressional pages, or playing footsie in airport bathroom stalls? I think of this practice as Shakespeare's "The Lady Doth Protest Too Much" Syndrome.

The Handheld Mirror

Earlier we saw an illustration of the ego with the handheld mirror it uses to look into the past. It also uses that same mirror as a weapon to prove it is always right. The ego shoves it in people's faces so they can see the folly of their ways or how wrong they are. "See, you always do that!"

The problem with projection is that it disempowers and keeps us trapped in the muck of victim consciousness. Doing the work of reeling in our projections is particularly difficult because, by definition, a blind spot is hard to see. It is much easier to blame *them*, to make it about *them*. We make wrong over *there* what we cannot accept over *here*.

As long as we do that, however, we keep the area in need of healing in the realm of the unconscious. We remain unable to see our blind spots. No growth will happen and no healing either, as long as we are holding someone else responsible. And, as the saying goes, whenever there is a pointed finger of blame, as we see in the illustration, look closely and you'll see three pointing back at you.

Some years ago, I took my mom on a cruise from Rio de Janeiro to Buenos Aires and we shared a cabin. Mistake number one! I knew better; I know I need my space and alone time to maintain center and equanimity. My mom does not travel lightly, so I'm schlepping her bags and pillows as well as my stuff in and out of cars and airplanes and through narrow hallways on the ship. I'm not sleeping well. She has sleep apnea, so with her CPAP machine it felt like I was sharing a room with Darth Vader. She is also overweight and diabetic and as I watch her go to town on the buffets, I am consciously having to exert self-discipline, reminding myself that the trip was my idea, that I am paying for the whole thing, and that I knew what kind of food is served on cruises. I walk my talk, practice the teachings and am fully aware of personal accountability, but it's taking intentional effort not to say anything. The pressure builds as two outings get canceled due to weather or mechanical problems; there is no rest for the weary and no relief in sight. I am still not sleeping well and have not had time to myself.

We finally arrive in Buenos Aires and because we are using my miles to fly back and forth, we end up staying two extra nights to make the schedule work. On the last day, we go to the famous flea market in Recoleta, and she sees this ring she has to have. She didn't have enough cash, I didn't have enough cash, and this is before the days of Square and Apple Pay. The story could have ended here, but I hear these words come out of my mouth: "Well, I do have an emergency stash back at the apartment"—not thinking that any rational human being would want to dip into an emergency stash. But she goes, "Oh, OK!" Somewhat befuddled, not understanding what part of *emergency* stash is unclear, I am still well aware that I have a choice and can say no. But I override that. It's my mom, and I would need another book series to tell the stories of how many sacrifices she and my dad made for their nine kids. Tired, not sleeping well, no time alone . . . add to that time pressure and now we have a recipe for a perfect storm! Now we have to go clear across town to get the damn ring before heading to dinner before going elsewhere for a tango show.

Back at the apartment, I'm doing my best to maintain patience while keeping an eye on the time. I remind her several times,

"Mom, we have to go." But alas, she moves slowly at this point in her life. We manage to make it to the flea market while the vendor is still open. With the ring in hand I get back in the cab and to this day, I can't recall what she said . . . but that was it. Volcanic eruption, inspired by an image of a shark feeding frenzy I once witnessed at the Miami Seaquarium.

"You have been in an eating frenzy and a shopping frenzy all week! You have no self-discipline!" I have enough presence and self-awareness to be doing the cycle of react and regret in the moment. As I vomit the suppressed words, I'm already regretting them: *How could I say such mean things to my mom?*

She was great about it though, and did not defend or explain herself but merely said, "Yes, you're right."

Of course, now she's happy with the big old ring on her finger! I'm actually grateful I got it because we later realized it was her anniversary, and my dad always used to give her jewelry on that day when he was alive. Plus, I've gotten great mileage from the story!

Because here is where it gets really interesting. Flash forward a few months, and I'm in New York when I get a text from my friend Holly, who is a personal shopper. "Hey, I saw you're in town and want to gift you with a half-day of personal shopping."

"Hmm," I think, "I actually need some new stuff for work, for professional speaking engagements." $500 max, I tell myself. $4,000 later (I should have known a personal shopper was not going to take me to Nordstrom Rack or Ross Dress for Less), I'm sitting numb and overwhelmed at my friend's place surrounded by shopping bags. This is more than I have spent in clothing in probably 20 years! It actually turned out to be $3,000; there was a $1,000 leather jacket I returned because I just couldn't keep it. But at this point in the story, it's still the full amount. Not knowing what else to do, I call my mom, the shopaholic, thinking she'd appreciate hearing about my purchases. As I'm telling her "I got this and that and the other thing," she must have been waiting patiently for just the perfect moment. Either that or in a flash of brilliance or divine inspiration, she quietly, daintily, drops the bomb: "Oh, so *you* got the frenzy!" Bam! Busted. What's over there at the end of the pointed finger is also here. I just have it much better managed!

Reeling in our projections is the stuff of heroes. We also learn the practice of turning the mirror around: "If it's there, it's here!" "How do I do that?" We will cover this dynamic more in depth in the next book on relationships. For now, we begin to set the stage by noticing our projections, expanding our perceptions, and beginning to soften our judgments.

An important part of the work of self-knowledge, then, is understanding our kinks and weaknesses. Our buttons. Because, to be sure, others will identify them and go for the jugular in a power skirmish or fight. Then they've got us. We are completely in their clutches.

## HEALTHY REFLECTIONS

Because of the nature of blind spots, clear feedback from an outside source—such as a therapist, counselor, or coach—is helpful. Or even a good friend who won't take your side reflexively and commiserate: "Poor you. How could that savage treat you that way?" "That bitch said that to you?" Instead, you need someone who will hold you to your highest ideals. That is work of the highest compassion, though it might seem coldhearted in the moment. Busting ourselves on our ego tendencies is nothing less than heroic work. It is challenging and immensely rewarding—and a key to freedom.

## POWER PRACTICES

- Tell someone a story of a recent upset, or just tell it while recording it on your phone. Don't be nice and sweet and all spiritual about it. Let it rip. Let all the harsh and nasty judgments out. Then retell it in third person. For example, in round one I might say "That SOB Brett had the gall to embarrass me in public. In the middle of my story he interrupts me and humiliates me by contradicting what I said. When I corrected him, he practically calls me a liar. Can you believe that?" The retelling might sound like "Christian is in the middle of telling a story from childhood. His friend Brett interrupts to add some information. Christian then says: "I don't think that's how it happened." Brett responds: "Well, that's how I remember it." How does that feel different?

- Ponder and create a list:

  - Which button got triggered in me? Why does that upset me?

  - In which situations and with what type of person do I feel off my game?

  - How do I feel when that happens?

  - What previous similar situations does that remind me of?

  - When else have I felt that way?

  - What patterns begin to emerge?

# Chapter 9
## Keys to Breaking Free

What a tragic state of affairs, living the ego's way! Talk about a self-made prison. The good news is that because it is self-made, we can make the choice to break free and liberate ourselves. We are our own jailers, and no one can keep us in there against our will.

How do we break free? And what is the goal?

### 1. Intention is the First Step

First, we must really want to be free. Breaking out of victim consciousness, for example, is nothing less than a heroic leap in evolution. But it must be done; it is the price to pay for freedom. (We will dive deeper into the victim later.)

### 2. Disidentify with the Ego

We are not our egos. The second step is to begin to disidentify with the baseball and reidentify with the stadium.

It helps to attribute what can be called lower tendencies—neediness, victim, self-deprecation, bossiness, manipulativeness, self-righteousness, control issues—to this small and wounded part of who we are. Pay attention when these rear up. Instead of taking everything so personally and getting all worked up about what a great injustice was just done to us, tell yourself: "My ego just got triggered" and begin to disidentify with that.

## 3. MINDFUL AND RELENTLESS VIGILANCE

It has now been more than thirty years since I was first exposed to these teachings about the ego, and they dramatically changed my life. Quickly. Within months I was teaching them to others. Since then I have taught them on too many occasions to count.

Though I still have an ego, it rarely gets triggered these days. When it does, I hardly ever react. I see it coming, nip it in the bud, and bring choice into the equation: How do I want to respond to that? On the rare occasion when the ego gets me and I react, I go in and out of the experience and quickly clean it up. Sometimes I let things brew overnight or even a couple of days, to make sure I'm not coming from a reactive place. When necessary, I reach out to a trusted and credible advisor for mirroring, someone who understands the nuances of the process and is equally committed to transcending the ego in their lives.

At one time I might have gotten stuck in self-righteousness for a week or longer, as I waited for the other person (who was obviously at fault, inevitably in the wrong, and of course should make amends or correct the situation!) to take the first step. Or I might have crucified them—crossed them out of my life. (Is this not a form of modern-day crucifixion?) As I got practiced transcending the ego more deeply with a former partner who was also committed to the process, after some time we'd navigate the upset within a couple of days. Eventually, we could work through our stuff in a couple of hours. At times, we were able to handle the conflict, attain resolution and get to a place of healing in the moment.

In the next book on relationships (and in the Soulful Relationships retreats)

we will better explore how having a willing partner to do the work of self-analysis, reclaiming projections, and busting one's own ego tremendously expedites the growth process.

And yet it's not all smooth sailing. The farther we go on the spiritual path, the sneakier the ego gets and the more subtle its machinations. Maia, my teacher, used to speak of this phenomenon as the spiritualized ego. The ego learns the spiritual language and concepts and figures out how to come across as evolved and spiritual—but what it's actually doing is using the very same teachings as weapons, to win or be right.

When I was in the ashram, for example, in a setting in which all of us were supposed to be living the teachings, I witnessed an argument ensue between two disciples. One of them stood with crossed arms accusing the other one: "You are just being your ego right now!" True, but what was the other doing, acting so smug, separate, and self-righteous? That too is ego.

Maintaining constant vigilance is a necessary and ongoing third step. Ultimately, with awareness and practice, the ego grabs us less frequently, and when it does, we spend less and less time in its grip.

## 4. CHOICE

The ego is reactive. Whenever one of its buttons gets pushed, it gets triggered and all wound up and fights back, likely pushing one of the other person's buttons in return. But then, after the adrenaline dissipates a bit, it typically slips into regretting what it did or said. "That was so mean, what I said to Daisy; I wish I hadn't said it that way. I'm such a bad person." We all have gotten stuck in those tired and boring React and Regret cycles for much of our lives. Introducing choice into the equation is the fourth step.

How do we break the cycle of React and Regret? Part of getting free requires that we own that it's our stuff—our buttons, our pain, our anger. Consider this example: Ryan, Amber, and Lorena have a date for lunch. After 45 minutes of waiting for Ryan, Amber is getting increasingly angry and upset by his lateness and the fact that he hasn't communicated with them. Lorena is relaxed, enjoying her time with Amber. When Ryan finally arrives, with halfhearted apologies about traffic, Amber can't hold herself back and cracks a joke—"That's the reason you can't keep a relationship!"—knowing that he recently broke up with his girlfriend. They navigate their lunch, but the undertow of hurt, anger, and discomfort are palpable beneath the surface. Ryan feels guilty, and though he is trying to put on a brave face, he has plummeted into feelings of failure. Amber walks away feeling worse, knowing that underneath her attempt at humor, what she said to Ryan was hurtful and mean-spirited. She also knows that she didn't really face the situation head on but instead took the easier way out by means of a barbed and loaded cruel joke.

It is interesting to note the difference in response between the two women. Lorena has other buttons, to be sure, but not this particular one. She seemed to enjoy her time with Amber as they waited for Ryan. Amber, on the other hand, has a history of not feeling valued and respected by men, stemming from her relationship with her father, a prescription drug addict who drifted in and out of her life. Ryan's lack of consideration triggered her unworthiness button. When she was a little girl, Amber mistakenly concluded that her father didn't love her, and misinterpreted his absence to mean that it was her fault, that there was something wrong with her because he didn't love her. This was not true, of course, but rather, a misunderstanding of a young mind that did not know any better. Though it has no basis in reality, that unhealed wound has been impacting all her subsequent relationships, especially those with men.

While none of this means that Ryan's lack of communication and inconsiderate behavior are acceptable, Amber has choices to make as to how to handle the situation going forward. She can learn how to communicate to Ryan what works and doesn't work for her and the effect his behavior has on her. She can negotiate outcomes with him and if worse comes to worst, she can walk away from the relationship. One effective approach is to say something to Ryan like, "Ryan, I appreciate our friendship and love our weekly lunches, but whenever you show up late, I feel disrespected and unappreciated, as if you value your time more than you do mine. I don't like feeling that way. Can't we do this a different way?" Note that she is approaching it from a place of vulnerability, which is actually a powerful stance. She is also not trying to control his behavior or tell him what to do. She's not giving his ego any ultimatums or accusing him in any way. She's simply pointing out the effect of his actions on her in a personal way and asking for his participation in changing a situation that does not work for her.

But the important thing for her is to heal the core issue. That means if she wants to get free, she needs to focus on her own worthiness button. Otherwise, Amber will always be subject to the actions of others who at some point may trigger her deep-rooted feelings of not being worthy of love and respect, and she will continue attracting people who will reflect that back to her. However, the heroic act of owning her anger and her unhealed past, which got activated by Ryan's boorish behavior, opened the door to her healing.

So first we own that it's our button, our issue to be healed. The goal is bringing in awareness and choice back into the equation, so we are not simply reacting subconsciously to old unresolved hurts. Too often when people figure out they can get a rise out of us by showing up late, for example, they have us under their influence. When we play along, we have potentially handed over our power. That's what happens in most relationships: We discover and push each other's buttons when we fight. Resentment builds up and trust goes out the window. Unaddressed, the prognosis for such relationships is not good.

To free ourselves we approach the situation from two levels. First, we try cognitively to understand the source of our patterns and hang-ups. We get to know ourselves and do whatever self-esteem work we need to do. Second, we use the powerful effects of breathwork in healing those old wounds and traumas at the source, permanently, so that when someone tries to push the button, nothing happens. That powerful one-two punch is exactly what takes place in Soulful Power workshops and retreats, with extraordinary effects. More on this shortly.

Our job then, is to flatten our buttons so no one can trigger us. That's freedom. And nothing less than heroic work.

## POWER PRACTICES

- Now that you have a better perspective of the ego, how does it show up in your life? Where does it wreak the most havoc? What triggers it? What patterns are you noticing?

- Write your own Hero Pledge, your declaration of emancipation. Following is an example of a personal statement of emancipation you might adapt and make yours, as a way to declare your intention.

Sample Declaration of Personal Emancipation:

I declare myself free from the tyranny of the ego, from the need to defend, from the need to explain who I am, from victim consciousness, from addictive tendencies. I reclaim power over my body, mind, and spirit. I always have a choice about how to show up in response to any situation. I am master of my life. I no longer allow fear to determine my choices. I surrender to the highest good without attachment to outcome. I let go of thinking that I need to know the timeline in which things should unfold. I let go of resistance, holding back, and playing small.

Revamp that declaration and add some of your own proclamations.

# CHAPTER 10
## ON THE WAY TO FREEDOM

We have now seen the many traps in the Empire of the Ego: the Impregnable Jungle of Defensiveness, the Decoy of Projection, The Lure of Greed, The Labyrinth of the Monkey Mind, The Vast Desert of Lack, Judgment Bay, The Abyss of Arrogance, the Swamp of Self-righteousness, the Trap of Reactivity, the Tar Pits of Guilt, the Swamp of React and Regret, the Pitfall of Victimhood, the Marsh of Manipulation, the Quagmire of Unworthiness, the Forbidden Forest of Fear of Failure.

So many pitfalls, but thankfully, there is a way out. We have some powerful allies, guardians, and protectors to guide us and keep us on the path to freedom.

THE WAY IN IS THE WAY OUT.

**Self-awareness** keeps us honest and from falling into traps. The way in is the way out.

**Choice** and **personal responsibility** are keys to freedom and keep us out of the prison of victimhood.

**Compassion** makes possible **forgiveness**, and enables the process of healing ourselves and our pasts.

## How Do We Solve a Problem Like the Ego?

We can trace both interpersonal and international conflict directly back to the ego. It is the source of our feelings of separation and alienation, of all suffering, ultimately. Some Kabbalah teachings refer to Satan as the ego. In his lighthearted *Satan: An Autobiography*, for example, Yehuda Berg also refers to the ego as a "stunt double" and as our "reactive response to the world."[6]

As cunning, insidious, and manipulative as the ego is, does that mean that it is evil and should be destroyed? Or could the ego be completely transcended while we are in body, so that we never get triggered again? I don't know for sure. My understanding is that as long as we are in a body, in third-dimensional reality, we need to have an ego serving as a fulcrum for consciousness. What I do know is that it is very doable to live a life that is not governed by it, that we can free ourselves from its fearful and neurotic hold on us, so that it seldom gets triggered. When it does, we are able to choose our response and transcend its reactive nature. In a sense, the hypothetical, philosophical question of whether the ego can be left completely behind is not important. What matters is that we get free. The essential goal is that we learn to manage our egos. That's what heroes do.

In Maia Dhyan's words, "Our goal is to remove the ego from the place it has hijacked as the sun, placing it in its proper place in orbit around and in service to the sun." In other words, we no longer allow it to run the show.

Even Gollum retains traces of his "humanity," his authentic hobbit nature. He is a tragic character deserving of compassion. And, like Gollum, the ego is way over its head. It experiences itself in a constant state of overwhelm, feeling responsible for and unsuccessfully trying to control and micromanage every aspect of our lives—and everyone else's as well. A futile and pitiful effort to control the uncontrollable! No wonder it often slips into feeling helpless and hopeless. Talk about Atlas feeling the weight of the world on his shoulders.

While the ego may put up a façade that it's tough and capable, deep down it feels like a fraud, an imposter. Underneath the bravado, it feels weak and damaged, incapable, and incompetent. So when we reclaim our rightful central role and demote the ego to its proper place in orbit around the sun, when we allow it to heal and place it back in proper alignment, we actually liberate the ego as well, to do the things it's good at doing.

Ah, you mean the ego isn't all bad? That's right. The ego can make sense of sensory information that would otherwise be overwhelming. It is a great organizer that can weave that information in with our past experiences and projections of future possibilities to create a coherent sense of self. Besides providing a sense of identity, the ego has other functions, such as efficient planning and strategizing.

American spiritual teacher and author Adyashanti compares the ego to a character in a novel: "When you read a novel, every character has a point of view. It has beliefs. It has opinions. There's something that makes it distinct from other characters. Our persona is literally this mind-created character that's always making itself distinct.... That's basically what it means to really wake up: we're waking up from the character. You don't have to destroy the character called "me" to wake up from it. In fact, trying to destroy the character makes it very hard to wake up. Because what's trying to destroy the character? The character. What's judging the character? The character."

What does the healed ego look like and what does the stadium represent? Beloved teacher and world-renowned author Ram Dass, who recently made his transition, frames it in way that connects back to our stadium metaphor:

"Your ego is a set of thoughts that define your universe. It's like a familiar room built of thoughts; you see the universe through its windows. You are secure in it, but to the extent that you are afraid to venture outside, it has become a prison. Your ego has you conned. You believe you need its specific thoughts to survive. The ego controls you through your fear of loss of identity. To give up these thoughts, it seems, would annihilate you, and so you cling to them.... There is an alternative. You needn't destroy the ego to escape its tyranny. You can keep this familiar room to use as you wish, and you can be free to come and go. First you need to know that you are infinitely more than the ego room by which you define yourself. Once you know this, you have the power to change the ego from prison to home base."

In the same way that the stadium needs a baseball in order to serve its purpose, we need an ego to function in a body. Instead of trying to get rid of the ego, we learn to become more aware of it—something that is simpler said than done, as the ego is very crafty and cunning! And the more knowledge we have, the more insidious it gets and the more subtle its expression.

Let's take a deeper look at the process of healing the ego.

## POWER PRACTICE

Deepening Your Inner Listening

- Perhaps you are feeling plateaued, stagnant, or even trapped by a situation in your personal or professional life. Often the ego, whose job it is to maintain the status quo, will ignore the inner messages or numb out the feelings of unease or dissatisfaction. How do we learn to override that and listen to the inner voice, even when it might be prodding us to make a change that feels scary? Take a break today. Pause. Find a quiet place where you can sit comfortably for a bit. Relax. Trust that you will be able to handle any outcome, that you are greater than any circumstance in your life. As you allow the breath to slow down and deepen, feel yourself dropping into your body and feeling safe. Allow the question and situation to come to mind and then let it go. Just observe whatever thoughts and sensations surface. Make some notes in your journal. Even when change is scary (to the ego), learning to listen to the inner voice and then following its guidance is the path to freedom, inner peace, and personal empowerment.

The Healed Ego

# CHAPTER 11
## HEALING THE EGO

We need to develop a strong sense of self before we can transcend it. I like the way Jeff Brown, author of *Grounded Spirituality,* writes about this on Facebook: "When I had a terrible self-concept, I could never admit I was imperfect or that I was wrong. My healthy ego was not developed yet, so admitting my shadow was too much to bear. I so wanted to see something good about me, after a childhood of negative feedback. It's important to remember that people often cannot acknowledge their flaws and mistakes, because their self-concepts are not strong enough to handle the admissions. Swimming in a pool of self-hatred, they can't take one more drop of contempt. After working hard to work through my shame-body—healing it, and proving my value with various achievements—it became a lot easier to admit my shadow characteristics, my mistakes, my arrogance. And, then, because my issues were more transparent, I could actually begin the journey of working them through. This is why the ego bashing intrinsic to the shadow jumping spiritual community is a dangerous thing. It confuses people and discourages them from developing the healthy ego necessary to manage reality and value themselves. We need a certain degree of egoic strength to evolve and flourish. Kudos to the healthy self-concept. Really."

In other words, while we're in the process of transcending the ego and illuminating our stadium nature—that is, our higher selves—

79

we can't jump over the shadow stuff and expect that it's just going to go away with a few OMs and "love and light" affirmations. We can't namaste the shadow away.

> WE CAN'T NAMASTE THE
> SHADOW AWAY.

We have to be willing to wrestle with our own egos as we reclaim control over our lives and engage in the challenging work of doing whatever we must to allow the ego to heal—to flatten its buttons so that anyone can push them and nothing happens. That's the stuff of heroes.

So, if we're not going to kill the ego, what do we do about it? What are we working toward? What might a healed ego, a healthy ego, look like?

## THE HEALED EGO

As the image illustrates, the ego's scars have been healed and its buttons flattened. It has released its tight grip, and its hands are now open and free. It has realized its proper place in orbit around the sun, rather than thinking it is the sun. Its need to control everyone and everything has dissipated, and it has relaxed into living in a state of trust and going with the flow. No longer does it have a paranoid me-against-the-world mentality. It has realized that it requires a lot of energy to maintain a permanent state of fuck you. It stands free. Instead, it might even be established in a state of *pronoia*, the belief that the Universe conspires to support it.

We note too that, through our work, it has been able to lay down its masks and weapons of happiness destruction, which now lay strewn all around. The bag of the past is on the floor, empty. Through breathwork or other modalities, unresolved issues have been cleared and stuffed emotions from the past released. The ego is able to remember and learn from past experiences but is no longer stuck reacting to situations that no longer exist.

Its old armor has also been removed. The ego has been aligned with the higher self and now realizes it is safe to take down the defenses that may have served a purpose at some point, but which are no longer needed.

In fact, those old coping mechanisms have been interfering with our ability to be happy. They have been wreaking havoc in our relationships, not to mention the amount of energy it takes and the price we pay to maintain a constant state of DEFCON 1. Letting down the defense shields is liberating in many ways. We have freed ourselves from our self-made prison and discovered the power of vulnerability, allowing the deeper and more subtle aspects of ourselves to shine through.

The healed ego's eyes are now wide open; with the ego receiving a reality check, we now see ourselves and reality more clearly. The healed ego's mouth and ears are now proportionate.

The healed ego has finally learned that it has nothing to prove. It has healed whatever old messages of misunderstandings from the past had kept it in cycles of overcompensation for feelings of not being good enough. With that old stuff cleared and a strong sense of self in place, no longer is the ego driven by the need to be right. This openness makes room for more fair, considerate, and open-minded interactions with others. With self-acceptance and self-esteem in place, there is no longer need for overcompensation and grandiosity, and the habitual demanding, strict, rigid, and punitive ways begin to fall away. We learn to forgive and let everyone, including ourselves, off the cross of perfectionism. With personal accountability in place, we never again feel like victims and no longer blame others for our state of being.

The healed ego now stands in an attitude of empowered surrender. One pair of hands rests downward, palms open in receptive mode, in a confident, free, and defenseless stance: "I can handle any situation that comes my way." Another pair of hands rises overhead in a symbol of victory and freedom: the victim has been transformed into victor. The third pair is in prayer form, in a state of constant gratitude and empowered humility, honoring all creation.

Having removed the ego from its self-appointed place as the sun, we are now aligned with the Soulful Self, which allows us to feel once again connected, reverent, humble, living in a state of gratitude. No longer do we feel separate and alone, and we are never lonely. We realize that those old feelings of alienation and abandonment were just illusion. Guilt, hopelessness, and helplessness can exist only in the realm of the ego.

We are able to express ourselves with authentic power and radical honesty. We are free to be who were at all times and all situations. We learn to express our truth responsibly, with courage, gracefulness, and compassion, mastering clear communication and congruent self-expression. What we say matches how we feel inside.

A new and trusting relationship to life means that we no longer feel limited or stuck in lack, which allows our innate generosity to come forth. With no more issues of worthiness at play, we learn to live in balance and in accordance with an abundant universe. No longer stuck in fear and limitation, we live in a reality in which miracles are commonplace. Taking on the practice of bringing ourselves in from the past and back from the future, we find ourselves increasingly present and self-aware.

With renewed focus and intention, we strive for personal excellence, but with joy and with nothing to prove, always balancing self-care. We have learned to honor ourselves and our needs, and we attract people into our lives who also do so. We can now appreciate simple living and enjoying the gifts of the present moment, responding spontaneously to needs that show up. There is no need for validation. Our sense of worth is internally referenced, and established: "I know who I am, and I am that in different settings and in every situation, courageously and unapologetically."

From time to time the ego will feel triggered and the old habitual defensiveness will get activated, but it happens less and less frequently, and when it does, we spend less time stuck in it.

## POWER TOOLS FOR HEALING THE EGO

Sounds great, doesn't it? Who wouldn't want to transform their lives and live that way? Here are three powerful tools to start your journey toward healing your ego today.

1. **Mindful self-observation.** With practice, self-discipline, and commitment, we develop the ability to unyieldingly, but compassionately, bust ourselves on our egoic tendencies, no longer giving in to its tactics and machinations. We learn to be as patient and focused as the puma stalking its prey.

2. **Breathwork.** In my experience, nothing is more effective or quicker in healing past trauma and clearing suppressed and accumulated emotional crap.

3. **Meditation.** Most of the time, when we sit in meditation practice, it is pretty boring. We observe our breath or repeat our mantra and then a few minutes later realize we have been thinking about a project at work. We dutifully bring our attention back to the breath. A few moments later we realize that we have been working on our shopping list for dinner. We bring our attention back to the breath. Soon after that, we catch ourselves planning a response to the argument we had last night with our partner. Once again, we bring our attention back to the breath. Most of the time, meditation is like that, nothing fancy. Once in a while we experience exquisite moments of no-mind, expanded states of consciousness, or a sense of connectedness to all creation. Those are great when they happen. Most of the time it's no bells and whistles, no choirs of angels, no flashiness or frills. But the humble practice of regular sitting is like training for a triathlon or a piano recital. Months of training and preparation finally come together as reflexes, experiences, and practice coalesce. When the rubber hits the road and we are about to get hijacked by the ego, that's when those hours of self-observation come

into play: "Oh, my ego just got triggered! How do I want to be with this?" Meditation trains us to develop witness consciousness, the ability to observe ourselves as if from above, making choice possible.

## POWER PRACTICE

Self-observation is an indispensable power tool for heroes.

- Set your timer for an interval of your choice, for example, every hour. Once it goes off, pause whatever you are doing (whenever possible) and take a few deep breaths. What's going in your body? Are you feeling tired, sore? Scan your body and note any physical sensations. What thoughts were just running through your mind? Were you thinking about a project? Daydreaming about your date tonight? Were they positive, worrisome, or perhaps fearful thoughts? Were you deep in a memory or fantasizing about a possible future occurrence? And what are you feeling right now? What kind of emotional energies are coursing through your body: Sadness? Anger? Joy? Keep notes in your journal and see if notice any patterns.

# CHAPTER 12
## THE SOULFUL SELF

I n the metaphor of the ego and the sun, the sun represents the Higher Self, the Authentic Self—in contrast to our Pseudo Self, our ego's extremely limited sense of self. Call it the soul, the spirit in us. Our own small parcel of the Divine, our own piece of sacred real estate.

The healthy ego, now realigned in orbit around and in service to the sun, enables us to be a force for good in the world. It helps bring forth and implement the Soulful Self's passion to contribute, to make a difference in the world. In contrast to the unhealed ego's judgmental nature, the Soulful Self is passionate and compassionate. It evaluates and discerns, instead of judging. Whereas the unhealed ego felt separate and lonely, the Soulful Self is always aware of its connection to the Universe. It thrives on excellence, rather than being driven by perfectionism. It allows room for mistakes, as part and parcel of the learning process. It is constant, not fickle. If the unhealed ego was fearful and fear-based, the Higher Self is courageous. It is courage itself—an open heart, no matter what.

> THE SOULFUL SELF IS OUR OWN SMALL PARCEL OF THE DIVINE, OUR OWN PIECE OF SACRED REAL ESTATE.

## YOU'RE NOT ALONE

As we have seen, fear of abandonment and a sense of mortality are part of the price we pay for having an individual sense of self. How do we regain sense of connection while in a body and still having a persona? Certain meditative practices, such as breathwork or shamanic states, can lead to transcendent experiences of unitary consciousness, when we feel a sense of belonging and interconnectedness, an experience of being a part of it all. Such moments help us realize that abandonment and loneliness are illusions of the ego. Ultimately, the truth is we can't be alone even if we wanted to. We also realize that it is the flimsiest of veils separating us from other realms of being. Often, in breathwork, people will have an experience of connecting with loved ones who are no longer embodied. These types of experiences help the ego feel connected and realize that it no longer has to feel separate and lonely.

After surviving a serious cycling accident, filmmaker Tom Shadyac, who produced most of Jim Carrey's comedies, set out to explore what's wrong with the world and what we can do it about it. I won't spoil how he beautifully wraps up those questions at the end of his brilliant documentary *I Am*, but one of the powerful messages it reveals in the process is cutting-edge research about the heart. As it turns out, the heart has a more powerful energy field than the brain. (Scientifically measurable—we're not talking auras here!) In one experiment conducted at the HeartMath Institute north of Santa Cruz, California, Tom is sitting at a table across from a bowl of yogurt, into which they have placed electrodes measuring electrical response. There is no direct physical connection between him and the yogurt. When asked questions with a high emotional content, such as "How is your marriage going?" or "Have you spoken to your attorney lately?", the yogurt has a response! If our unspoken emotions have a measurable effect on the bacteria in a bowl of yogurt, how can we

> "ONENESS NOT AS AN EQUIVALENCY OF BEING BUT A COMPLETE, MUTUAL INDWELLING: I AM IN GOD AND GOD IS IN ME."
> —CYNTHIA BOURGEAULT

not be connected to each other? What used to be pretty, poetic, and woo-woo spiritual stuff is now backed up by science. When we further consider the interconnectedness of the fabric of life, we realize that we are never alone and cannot be abandoned.

## HOW DO WE KNOW WHO'S WHO?

Because our ego, even when healthy, can slip into its old patterns, we need to remain constantly watchful. Toward that end, how can we tell whether that voice in our heads is the ego or our Higher Self? How do we know the difference, for example, between stubborn, egoic, prideful self-righteousness and a courageous, righteous stand for ourselves, for truth, for something we value?

This is not always easy; a lot depends on the come-from. But even that can be tough to figure out. The ego is brilliant and tricky, an expert at rationalizing, and the higher we go on the spiritual path the more subtle it becomes. Here are some ways to help us discern the difference.

As Maia Dhyan's *A Call to Greatness* brings to light, the ego uses big words, complex thoughts, and complicated arguments. It went to law school and is always building a case to prove that it's right. In contrast, the Soulful Self uses simple language. Its messages are simple: "Yes. No. Do this. Don't go there!" We get in trouble when we override those intuitive feelings. The ego's voice is so loud and overwhelming, and we need to learn how to quiet that crazy monkey mind of ours enough so that we can drop in and hear the quiet voice of the Higher Self.

The ego is also fickle and grandiose. It will have an idea this week that "Now I know what I need to do with the rest of my life, and it is going to solve world hunger and make me a multi-gazillionaire in the process." Three months later, it gets bored and decides, "That's not working. Now, this is what I need to focus my energies on! This is gonna solve all my problems!" A year later, after we have bored and exhausted ourselves and a couple of projects have imploded, that still quiet voice inside continues signaling its simple and consistent message: "Do that!"

## THERE IS HOPE

We must cultivate our gardens. The work of self-healing, self-awareness, and ego transcendence is the most important journey any one of us could undertake. And it is not easy! Along the way, we will encounter inner demons in need of slaying, but we can do it. The inner journey toward self-understanding and self-mastery is the most heroic thing we can attempt.

This chapter ends with a hopeful conclusion to our feud story. In 1979, the Hatfield and McCoy descendants came together and played each other on the TV game show *Family Feud*. In addition to the customary cash prize, they competed for a pig that was kept on stage for the duration of the weeklong special. Two decades later in 2000, the families starting hosting joint family reunions. Their motto: "No feudin' . . . Just fun." In 2013 they officially signed a truce. Their annual gathering is now open to the public and features, among other activities, a marathon. The new motto: "No feudin' . . . Just runnin'." They even have a Hatfield McCoy Feud Tour App that guides tourists to the historical locations and sites and includes photos, GPS maps, and relevant historical documents.

So yes, there is hope. If the Hatfields and McCoys can find a way to resolve their differences, surely we can manage to bring peace to our relationships and harmony to our lives! There is a way out of the captivity of the ego. On that individual act of personal emancipation depends the fate of the world, the resolution of all interpersonal and international conflicts. As more and more of us become aware of what it is, how the unrealized ego holds us back and learn how to free ourselves from its stranglehold, the ripple effects will be felt throughout the world. Calling All Heroes!

Another quote from *A Course in Miracles* bookends this chapter:

> We cannot really make a definition for what the ego is, but we can say what it is not. And this is shown to us with perfect clarity. It is from this that we deduce all that the ego is.... Where there was darkness, now we see the light. What

is the ego? What the darkness was. Where is the ego? Where the darkness was. What is it now and where can it be found? Nothing and nowhere. Now the light has come: Its opposite has gone without a trace.... This was the ego—all the cruel hate, the need for vengeance and the cries of pain, the fear of dying and the urge to kill, the brotherless illusion and the self that seemed alone in all the universe.... Your questions have no answer, being made to still God's Voice, which asks of everyone one question only: "Are you ready yet to help Me save the world?"[7]

Maneuvering the Empire of the Ego is a journey for a lifetime. You now have the tools of understanding and the keys to freedom. You are encouraged to create the support systems, your own Power Pod, to help keep you on the journey, to keep you real and accountable. That is up to you.

The adventure continues . . . Now we are ready to enter the Zone of Power.

## POWER PRACTICE

- Who's on your team? The heroic journey described here will take you through ups and down, peaks and valleys, traps, and quagmires. Having your **Power Pod** of fellow travelers will make all the difference in challenging times and will provide opportunities for mutual support, accountability, and inspiration. Please join the **Unleash Your Inner Hero Group** on Facebook. There you will encounter others also committed to their journey of self-discovery and liberation. Are there others with whom you'd like to share a Power Pod? What name comes up to describe its participants? (Perhaps based on geography or a favorite theme? Examples: Peoria Power Pod, Truth Warriors Power Pod, SOBE Rainbow Power Pod.)

# PART III

## THE ZONE OF POWER

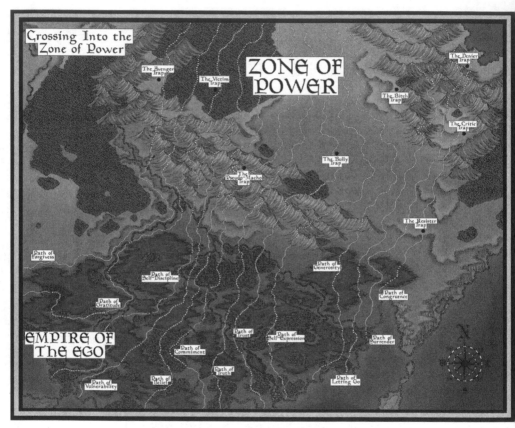

Zone of Power Map

# CHAPTER 13
## SOULFUL VS. EGOIC POWER

Have you ever felt that sense of dread that comes with knowing you're caught in a power struggle? First it grips your stomach . . . then your chest tightens up. Or maybe you feel your pulse quicken as your insides begin to cave. You know you are trapped in a power play when the pull of someone else's agenda yanks you off balance. It might be your boss or your spouse—even your teenager can turn into an opponent hell-bent on showing you who's boss.

And then there's that part of us that's instinctively defensive and responds: "You're not the boss of me! I'll show you who's got the power!" The tug-o-war that ensues can destroy relationships, ruin careers, and—when played out on the world stage—bring nations to the battlefield.

A power play is like a riptide. Anyone who has ever lived near the ocean knows the worst thing you can do is fight it and swim against it. You are sure to drown. Power can be like that. And yet, the neurology in our brain is hardwired to fight.

What if we were to learn another way of navigating power struggles? What if we were able to expand our repertoire when it comes to power and learn to maneuver power conflicts authentically and at choice, achieving our desired outcome without getting stuck in a cycle of "react and regret"?

There is much confusion in the world about power: what it is, who holds it, what it means, how it works. We have a push/

pull relationship with it: we want it but are afraid of abusing it. Perhaps the reason we are conflicted about power is that we are thinking about fundamentally different types of power.

Worldly or egoic power always has an agenda and is selfish or self-serving. It achieves its goals by force, domination, control or manipulation and is often abusive, arrogant, and self-aggrandizing. It is fear-based, exclusive, hierarchical, and tends to squelch others or push them down in order to feel powerful.

In contrast, soulful or spiritual power guides and inspires. It is humble, quiet, and unassuming; its source and energy are internal. Soulful power is about authentic self-expression, about service and making a difference. It is love-based, inclusive, and not threatened by others having power. It stands freely on its own. It simply is. And it is mighty.

As you continue on your hero's journey and find your way through what I call the Zone of Power, you will be inspired to engage with power in new ways that generate a deeper level of fulfillment, satisfaction, and effectiveness in the world. At the same time, you will develop your own expression of power that is congruent with the essence of who you are. The journey through the Zone of Power will teach you how to swim out of the riptide to safety and show you the ropes so you land on your legs, sprout some wings, and fly!

The way we embody, express, and relate to power impacts every area of our lives: work, politics, religion, personal and romantic relationships—the area in which most of us tend to forfeit our inner power. The information explored in this realm will shift your relationship to relationships and guide you to freedom.

## CROSSING INTO THE ZONE OF POWER

To get into the Zone of Power, the hero must first get across the fear of rejection and overcome the fear of conflict. (Notice the river and the chasm in the map.) To be able do that, the hero has to resolve any ambivalence about power they may harbor. Otherwise there won't be enough of a drive. The motivation to step into one's power has to exceed the fear of rejection or conflict. The first step in that journey is understanding the different types of power. For our purposes, we will explore two: worldly or egoic power and soulful or spiritual power.

Worldly power refers to the way the world looks at power. This is power filtered through the ego and all its schemes, stratagems, and machinations. Worldly power leaves us feeling empty in the long run. No doubt, it can buy us momentary comfort, pleasure, status, and the illusion of well-being. However, it is not deeply fulfilling or long-lasting. Because its source is illusory and inauthentic, we can also think of it as *pseudo-power*.

In contrast, soulful power is authentic power and stems from the deeper, authentic part of who we are. It is characterized by authentic self-expression. It stands on its own, not needing to exert itself over others. It just is.

The following Power Chart further highlights the differences between these two kinds of power.

| Egoic Power | Soulful Power |
|---|---|
| External Focus | Internal Focus |
| Self-Serving/Self-Aggrandizing | Service-Oriented/Humble |
| Hierarchical/Power Over | Horizontal/Power With |
| Fear/Control/Force | Guidance/Inspiration/Love |
| Machiavellian/Conniving/Mind-Based | Intuitive/Body-Based (Heart/Hara) |
| Abusive | Respectful |
| Exclusive | Inclusive |
| Reactive/Impulsive | Responsive/At Choice |

## EXTERNAL VS. INTERNAL

Egoic, worldly, or pseudo-power is externally focused and associated with fame, money, social status, or political and/or religious connections. Because its source is external and therefore depends on the perception and acknowledgment of others, it is fickle. Here today, gone tomorrow.

In contrast, soulful power is self-referencing; it doesn't depend on external recognition and its focus and source are internal. Its power stems from authentic self-expression, deep self-awareness, and a connection to self, nature and the sacred

The original *Star Wars* film conveys the message found in many other books and films in the hero genre: that authentic power, soulful power, is within. As Luke prepares for his one-in-a-million chance to destroy the Death Star by dropping the bomb in just the precise place at exactly the right moment, he hears the voice of Obi-Wan Kenobi, his Jedi Master, reminding him to "trust the Force." Fear and doubt are overcome by trusting the inner voice of intuition. The power of one can bring down an empire.

Likewise, in *The Wizard of Oz*, the Good Witch, tells Dorothy: "You've had the power all along, my dear!" This beloved story likewise follows the framework of the hero's journey; the yellow brick road represents the path to freedom and empowerment.

> "SEEK TO KNOW THE POWER THAT IS WITHIN YOU."
> —JOSEPH CAMPBELL

## SELF-SERVING VS. SERVICE-ORIENTED

Egoic or pseudo-power is selfish and self-serving, always has an agenda, and can blind itself to the effect its actions have on others. It can be abused for personal gain, to impose one's will on another, to control or manipulate a desired outcome. Worldly power is insatiable and greed-driven; its agenda generally involves gaining more power.

When we reencounter Kylo Ren in *Star Wars Episode IX, The Rise of Skywalker*, he remains under the influence of the Dark Side. Ever hungry for more power, when he finds out that Emperor

Palpatine, the former leader of the Galactic Empire, still lives, he feels compelled to destroy him. In the realm of worldly power, others having power is a threat to one's own power.

Soulful power has a broader perspective and tends to be self-less. Power here is pursued not as end in itself but as a means to service and making a difference.

In the same film, the following scene provides contrast. The heroes, Rey, Finn, and Poe have found the ship they needed to retrieve a wayfinder, a device to help them locate the hidden planet of the Sith, where Emperor Palpatine is hiding. In the process of exiting the ship, they encounter a Vexis, a giant armored snake, blocking their way. While Finn and Poe (typically male in this example), prepare to battle and shoot the enormous creature, Rey realizes it is injured. Though Rey wields incalculably greater power than her companions, she instead uses the Force to heal the snake's wound and it then retreats, allowing them easy passage. Soulful power is benevolent, unselfish, and generous.

In Book 3 of the series *Living Your True Purpose and Leading with Soul*, we dive deeper into service. For now, a quick note on this theme: Mirroring the different types of power are also different expressions of service. Rooted in the level of ego, pseudo-service tends to be conditional and often takes on a self-denying, victim quality that can result in burnout and resentment. Almost counterintuitively, authentic, empowered service includes taking care of oneself.

One must be grounded and open to become a clear conduit through which power can flow. The vessel must be firm, strong, and steady. It is not self-serving, but it is not self-denying either. Like the instructions we are given when flying, we must take care of ourselves by first putting on our oxygen mask, then helping others. I have to fill my vessel first so that I have something to give you.

Roberta, a retreat participant, had a subconscious pattern of doing stuff for others as a way to seek validation and acceptance. That kind of pseudo-service, or service with an expectation of receiving something in return, is never fulfilling and is usually frustrating. Most often, people stuck in this behavior pattern are not even communicating their expectations. During the retreat Roberta realized that for her, the pattern originated at a young age, when she became her alcoholic mother's problem solver and caretaker. As she became aware of this setup for conditional giving and the misunderstanding that she had to do something in order to receive another person's love, she began to reevaluate her relationship choices and develop healthier boundaries. After a couple of years practicing self-awareness and breathwork, she was able to heal her original wound that she was not enough to be loved just for who she was. From that point on, she was able to give and serve freely out of her innate generosity, no longer because she was seeking love and approval from others. Freedom!

> "POWER IS THE ABILITY TO DO GOOD THINGS FOR OTHERS."
> —BROOKE ASTOR

## SELF-AGGRANDIZING VS. HUMBLE

In its original Greek meaning, the word *hero* meant protector or defender. Throughout history our greatest heroes have been just that, warriors who fought, protected, and often gave their lives for their people, their communities, or their countries. Most often heroes were not known for their humility but rather, for vanity and arrogance. Odysseus, who spent years and numerous travails because of his arrogance, and Icarus, who flew too close to the sun on wings of feathers and wax, come to mind in literature. Military leader General Patton is another example of an arrogant hero, as is Napoleon, whose overconfident, impulsive, and disastrous invasion of Russia brought about the end of his empire. In fact, in both life and literature, one fairly constant defining factor of the hero is hubris, or pride—often the cause of their tragic mistake or downfall. As the saying goes, "Pride comes before the fall."

In *Beauty and the Beast*, perfect-bodied, golden boy Gaston loses Belle to a "beast" because of his obnoxious self-absorption and clueless pride. In the world of finance, both in film and real life, examples abound of success turning into overconfidence and a sense of indestructibility, leading to inevitable downfall: Gordon Gekko in *Wall Street*, Jordan Belfort in *Wolf of Wall Street*, the insider trading of Martha Stewart, and the fraudulent schemes of Enron and Bernie Madoff.

Relevant to our discussion about power, those who wield worldly power are like a turkey that puffs himself up to seem bigger, stronger, and more impressive for the mating dance. The turkeys in our society—too many politicians and evangelists, for example—are so full of themselves they fail to recognize and address the real needs of their communities. No wonder in the Harry Potter books Albus Dumbledore wisely says (via J.K. Rowling), "It is a curious thing . . . but perhaps those who are best suited to power are those who have never sought it."

In our celebrity-driven culture of selfies, instant social media notoriety, and fake and scripted "reality" TV, there is a desperate need for humility, for soulful power. This kind of power does not need external validation—or to prove anything to anybody. Those who have it are strong enough to resist the temptation to use their power for selfish ends or self-aggrandizement, or to the detriment of others. The person with soulful power is humble and recognizes the sacred duty and responsibility that accompanies that power. Think of Gandhi—or Gandalf—dressed simply in their monastic robes, possessed of immense power that they used only when absolutely necessary.

> "POWER DOESN'T HAVE TO SHOW OFF. POWER IS CONFIDENT, SELF-ASSURING, SELF-STARTING AND SELF-STOPPING, SELF-WARMING AND SELF-JUSTIFYING. WHEN YOU HAVE IT, YOU KNOW IT."
> —RALPH ELLISON

## HIERARCHICAL VS. HORIZONTAL

Worldly power originates from the basic misunderstanding that exerting influence or control over another is what makes us powerful. It is about *power over*, and most commonly depends on our being able to squelch or step on others to feel powerful. This encourages negative competition, a dog-eat-dog atmosphere, and the ongoing struggle to get on top of the heap.

Soulful power is horizontal; it is about *power with* rather than *power over*. It stands freely on its own and is not an overcompensation for subconscious or repressed feelings of powerlessness. It simply is. People possessed of authentic power do not abuse or seek to impose their agenda on anyone else. Neither do they need to establish their authority and disavow another of their sovereignty. Soulful power involves self-expression and authentic communication.

Cooperation is as intrinsic in nature as competition. In fact, as the documentary *I Am* points out, Charles Darwin used the well-known and often quoted phrase *survival of the fittest* twice in his classic book *The Descent of Man*, whereas he used the word *love* 95 times.

In the Arthurian legends, the knights met in Camelot at the iconic Round Table, which symbolized the equal status of all the members. Power with, not power over.

Again, in *Star Wars Episode IX*, Poe approaches Finn and openly shares the new Commander role he was bestowed by Princess Leia. "I can't do this without you," he tells his friend, in this scene revealing a more vulnerable and equalitarian aspect of power, unlike the incident with the snake above.

> "POWER OVER OTHERS IS WEAKNESS DISGUISED AS STRENGTH. TRUE POWER IS WITHIN, AND IT IS AVAILABLE TO YOU NOW."
> —ECKHART TOLLE

## FEAR/CONTROL/FORCE VS. GUIDANCE/ INSPIRATION/LOVE

Worldly power tends to control by fear, force, and intimidation. Its modus operandi involves overpowering others. This is clearly, and sadly, the way of the world. Fear underlies the actions of egoic power, which are frequently expressed with force. How many more wars will it take for us to learn that vengeance and violence only beget more of the same? It is more powerful, more courageous, to break the cycles of violent power.

The word *courage* comes from the French *coeur,* which means "heart." Soulful power comes from the heart. It is ultimately about love—not wimpy, airy-fairy, pseudo-love, but a fierce and powerful love that transcends all, including time and space. If there is one word we associate with heroism, it is courage. Interesting that one of the highest honors bestowed by the U.S. military is the Purple Heart. As Zeus says in the animated film *Hercules,* "A true hero isn't measured by the size of his strength, but by the size of his heart."

Soulful power is authentic and natural, and it does not seek to force its agenda on others—although those who have soulful power can certainly take a fierce and implacable stand in the face of injustice. Gandhi brought the British Empire—when it was at its pinnacle—to its knees with his spiritually based strategies of nonviolence.

Soulful power is persuasive, not coercive, and attains its ends by guidance and inspiration. Soulful power does not control or micromanage but flows with life's surprises and the unpredictability of human nature. Said simply: Authentic power is free and seeks to set others free.

One of the recurring themes in the X-Men movies is the fundamental conflict between Magneto and Charles Xavier. Though their ultimate goal is the same—they both want a world in which mutants can be free and prosper—they have diverging perspectives as to how to best attain that. Xavier's vision is to transform society's fear and mistrust of mutants so all can live peacefully in mutual tolerance and respect. Toward that end, his school strives to teach mutants how to master their powers responsibly and use them in service toward humanity. His philosophy then, is about *power with*—and acceptance through inspiration, service, and love.

Magneto's approach is more an expression of worldly power. To him, for mutants to use their powers to help the very same society that seeks to persecute and oppress them makes no sense.

His approach is more tribal in orientation and geared toward survival of the fittest: *power over* through superior force.

Comparably, in Julian May's science fiction series *The Saga of Pliocene Exile*, humanity has attained a level of evolution in which a certain number of humans have developed extraordinary powers, such as telepathy, psychokinesis, and psychic healing. To the rest of humanity, those with powers are viewed with fear and distrust; conflict inevitably ensues. At a crucial moment, a large number of the gifted ones are surrounded at a mountaintop retreat and are faced with an existential choice as armed militias approach with the intent of destroying them. While they know they can combine their power and obliterate the approaching forces, many feel that would be a misuse of their power. After much back and forth, they collectively decide not to use their power for violence. In that moment, thousands of spaceships intervene carrying advanced technologies that solve all of humanity's problems—hunger, disease, environmental imbalance—within a few years. We choose love, pass the test, and are inducted into galactic consciousness. (No spoilers; the series begins here.)

"WHEN THE POWER OF LOVE OVERCOMES THE LOVE OF POWER THE WORLD WILL KNOW PEACE."
—JIMI HENDRIX

## MANIPULATION/SCHEMING/MIND-BASED VS. INTUITIVE/BODY-BASED (HEART/HARA)

While egoic power tends to be associated with the mind and mental processes, soulful power resides more in the body—in the heart and gut. The language of the former consists of words and complex reasoning, whereas the latter stems from the simple language of intuition and feelings. Egoic power is all about grandiose ideas, complicated strategies, and Machiavellian schemes. Its covert world of calculated moves and hidden agendas is highly controlled, and its victims and casualties are numerous.

Egoic power also uses manipulation as a way to control others and to get what it wants. In a recent cartoon, a one-percenter corporate type in an expensive suit sits at a table with a dark-skinned, shabbily dressed immigrant and a poor, white, blue-collar type. The rich guy, sitting in front an overflowing plate of cookies, tells the white worker, who stares at the single cookie on his plate: "Careful, they're coming for your cookie." Worldly power is manipulative and divisive, using fear—of survival, lack, loneliness, or other threats—as its weapon.

In the *Star Wars* franchise, whether it's Darth Vader and the Empire or Emperor Palatine and the First Order, power is expressed though fear, force, and manipulation—the way all tyrants rule. In Episode IX, at the critical final battle when it seems the rebels are about to be obliterated by the immeasurably superior force of the First Order, Poe Dameron realizes that "The First Order wins by making us think we're alone. We're not." The way of the tyrant is one of separation and division. Despots win by making those they seek to control feel separate and alone, weak, and helpless in the face of entrenched power and overwhelming force. Once Poe sees through those manipulative strategies and gets through his crisis of doubt, suddenly thousands of spaceships materialize from hyperspace and the battle turns. There is power in trust, power in community.

The messages and language of soulful power tend to be simple, subtle, intuitive, and in the moment, such as "Use the Force, Luke!" In *The Lord of the Rings*, Frodo's power stems from his courage, persistence, loyalty, and his

"I USED TO WANT TO SAVE THE WORLD. TO END WAR AND BRING PEACE TO MANKIND. BUT THEN, I GLIMPSED THE DARKNESS THAT LIVES WITHIN THEIR LIGHT. AND I LEARNED THAT INSIDE EVERY ONE OF THEM, THERE WILL ALWAYS BE BOTH. A CHOICE EACH MUST MAKE FOR THEMSELVES. SOMETHING NO HERO WILL EVER DEFEAT. AND NOW I KNOW THAT ONLY LOVE CAN TRULY SAVE THE WORLD. SO, I STAY, I FIGHT, AND I GIVE, FOR THE WORLD I KNOW CAN BE."
—WONDER WOMAN

innate ability to trust his intuition, even when all evidence points to the contrary.

Wonder Woman totally kicks butt and reveals her strength, power, and single-minded focus—qualities we tend to ascribe to the masculine energies. Yet she also is fueled by feminine qualities, including a deep sense of empathy and compassion. She is informed by her inner guidance, her intuition, and is driven by a knowing of who she is—even when she doesn't yet know all of who she is. She remains connected to her heritage, her family of Amazons, and her mission, no matter the challenges, all of which she faces with the courage that comes from conviction. Ultimately, it is love that animates her power.

## ABUSIVE VS. RESPECTFUL

Egoic power is often abused or expressed in an excessively forceful fashion. Power imbalance and abuse are clearly presenting themselves for us to take a closer look. Abuse of power occurs when the person carrying it out has control of the circumstances in a situation whether through legal authority or sheer dominance. For example, Black Lives Matter demonstrations against police brutality and systemic racism in the U.S. and globally surfaced in response to unfair application of power.

The abuse of power is not the exclusive realm of politicians, police or the wealthy and may also be found, for example, among spiritual teachers or leaders. Regrettably, many incidents are reported of power leakage in teacher/student relationships. The vulnerability and openness that these relationships require can also be conducive to seduction of power. This is a disservice to the student and an abuse of power.

The way the U.S. expressed its power in the years after 9/11 is a clear example of abuse of power. Stemming from a fear-based, "me against the world" cowboy mentality, our response to that tragedy was overreactive and paranoid, in addition to greed-driven and self-interested. In a matter of months, we managed to squander the goodwill of the world and the opportunities—and responsibilities—presented by being the sole global superpower, turning ourselves into hated pariahs. Our arrogant, go-it-alone, my-way-or-the-highway attitude was reactive and impulsive, and in the long run, counterproductive. The truth is nobody likes a bully.

Soulful power has deep respect for the implications of power and is mindful about expressing it in accord with the needs of each circumstance. Good people managers (and parents) know how to calibrate messages and instructions so that different team members (and children) can better hear them. Sometimes a more authoritative and directive approach is needed. With another team member, a softer message is more effective. While the egoic approach is to point fingers and pull rank, soulful power invites response and participation—and is no less powerful. My former teacher Maia told a story about being at a gas station where the attendant was rude and aggressive. Instead of taking it as a personal attack or being nasty in return, she took a deep breath, paused, looked him in the eye, and simply but firmly said: "Excuse me, I don't want to be treated this way." The guy stopped in his tracks, looked at her, and she could feel his energy shift and entire behavior change.

> "POWER COMES NOT FROM THE BARREL OF A GUN, BUT FROM ONE'S AWARENESS OF HIS OR HER OWN CULTURAL STRENGTH AND THE UNLIMITED CAPACITY TO EMPATHIZE WITH, FEEL FOR, CARE, AND LOVE ONE'S BROTHERS AND SISTERS."
> —ADDISON GAYLE, JR.

## EXCLUSIVE VS. INCLUSIVE

Pseudo-power seeks to hoard power. It shares reluctantly when there is no other choice or when a particular alliance will benefit its own agenda. Its basic premise is one of fear and lack. Anyone else's expression of power, or their efforts to gain power, is viewed as a threat. It actively seeks to squelch those threats with preemptive action.

Worldly power is secretive, protected, and withholding of information, whereas soulful power is transparent and allows for the free flow of information and emotions. It does not shut down. While worldly power sees emotions as a weakness and lives as if under siege in a state of defensiveness, soulful power embraces vulnerability as strength. It is so secure in itself that there is no need to defend anything.

In fact, soulful power seeks to empower others. It understands that power is not a zero-sum game. It is confident and self-sufficient and knows that another's power does not diminish its own. It seeks to expand rather than limit power.

> "KNOWLEDGE IS POWER; AND POWER IS BEST SHARED AMONG FRIENDS."
> —OTIS CHANDLER

Soulful power functions on a basic premise of trust and openness and requires count-on-ability. It leads by example, walks the talk. It gives of itself and does not attempt to hoard.

## REACTIVE/IMPULSIVE VS RESPONSIVE/AT CHOICE

At the same time egoic power is planning and scheming, it tends to live in a stressful state of fear and defensiveness. This approach, which may result in impulsive reactivity, is often harmful and readily lends itself to abuse. Even the "preemptive strike" mentality is reactive, aimed at a perceived threat to its security or status. Reactivity frequently leads to regret and broken relationships.

Soulful power is restrained and mindful of its potential effects on others. Carefully evaluating options, it acts and responds from a place of choice, rather than an automatic reaction. This requires radical self-honesty, self-discipline, mindfulness, and a constant evaluation of motives. In the gas station example above, Maia could have reacted, matching the attendant's energy and rudeness. She could have complained to the manager or threatened to get him fired. The scene could have escalated into a messy confrontation, a power struggle between egos trying to one-up each other. Comfortable in who she was and not needing to exert power over the attendant, she was also clear about her boundaries. She understood that the guy's behavior ultimately had nothing to do with her, and she was able to give him the benefit of the doubt—maybe he was just having a bad day. She chose to intervene accordingly, letting him know that she did not want to be treated this way. She was not telling the other ego—who didn't even know it was an ego—what to do or not to do, as in: "You will NOT speak to me that way!" She did not insult or issue an ultimatum such as: "You either stop talking to me to that way or I'm going to go in there and make sure your nasty ass gets fired!" She simply communicated how she wanted to be treated in a calm yet firm request. Her strategy worked.

> "ULTIMATELY, THE ONLY POWER TO WHICH MAN SHOULD ASPIRE IS THAT WHICH HE EXERCISES OVER HIMSELF."
> —ELIE WIESEL

## POWER PRACTICES

- Capture in your journal a recent example of a situation in which you got caught in a power struggle. From the current awareness of egoic power and soulful power, what insights do you now have? How might you handle the situation differently today?

- What are your negative thoughts about power?

- What are your positive thoughts about power?

- Where are you selling out on your power? (In what areas of life? In which relationships?)

# CHAPTER 14
## DANGER! POWER TRAPS AHEAD

The goal on this journey to the power zone is not to set up an either/or dichotomy of power or to automatically demonize worldly power. Rather, the goal is to expand how we think about power and provide a different way of looking at it.

Power is not intrinsically evil or corrupting, good or bad. Our intent determines whether power has a constructive or destructive outcome. Where we come from and how we use power affects whether it is soulful or egoic. Nor are the trappings of power intrinsically bad: fame, money, notoriety, social status, influence, political connections can all be used for the betterment of the world as well as for selfish and exploitative purposes.

In his book *Kinds of Power*, James Hillman warns about setting up love as the antithesis to power. Power is not the enemy of love, he states, but is too often cast as the opposite of love, soul, goodness, and beauty. "The corruption begins not in power, but in the ignorance about it . . . Giving careful consideration to something, sustaining deep interest in it, isn't this love?"[8] Hillman goes on to point out that one of the problems with setting up this dichotomy is that many people end up renouncing power in order to become more "loving."

This helps us understand why so many of us have a conflicted, approach/avoidance, push/pull relationship to power. One of the more common themes surfacing among participants of Soulful

Power retreats is the fear that they might abuse power or cause harm if they step into their power. We want it, but are afraid of it.

There are times when worldly power is appropriate. A crisis situation, such as a fire alarm going off in a crowded room, would not be the time to survey the group: "Hmm. Let's see, how many of you wonderful souls think we should take this exit? Please raise your hand." A leader would quickly assess the situation and clearly and unapologetically direct people: "Here! Go this way!" Or, when caught in the middle of a political power play in a work situation for example, it would be helpful to be aware of the workings and strategies of worldly power. Used consciously, this kind of power is certainly efficient and achieves its ends. Understanding how worldly power works may help us get what we want in certain situations.

The questions are: How do we employ power with integrity, cautiously, and consciously, without bringing about harm to self or others? What risks do we take when we decide to play in its energetic field? How do we manage it without being grabbed by its seductive nature, without falling into one of its traps? As you make your way through the Empire of the Ego, always remain vigilant to its potential perils and pitfalls.

## POWER LENDS ITSELF TO ABUSE

Again, this seems to be the main concern underlying many people's ambivalence about or rejection of power. The more self-aware we are and the more consciously we live our lives, the less we will be subject to egoic or even unconscious tendencies, and the less likely, therefore, that we will abuse power.

The goal is to become more and more aware of what motivates us—the thoughts and emotions and patterns of behavior that determine our behavior—so that we are more and more able to choose how we want to be in any given situation, rather than react impulsively and automatically. Possibly we fear power because some time in the past we misused it by overreacting, lashing out and hurting others. Instead, we want to introduce the element of choice into every situation. Perhaps we cannot choose our feelings and emotions, but we can certainly choose how we are going to be and how we will respond when those emotions surface. The end goal is clear, and we will look more specifically at how we get there in the coming pages.

Hubris was, to the ancient Greeks, the worst of all crimes. As we saw earlier, it refers to excessive, blinding pride, often leading to one's downfall. How many more politicians or religious leaders do we need to witness falling into webs of their own making? Richard Nixon. Elliott Spitzer. Bill Clinton. John Edwards. Larry Craig. John Ensign. Mark Sanford. Jim Bakker. Jimmy Swaggart. Ted Haggard. Paul Manafort. Donald Trump.

The list goes on.

These men—and they are usually men—are not only hypocritical but also blindsided by their shadow projections, which leads them to live out their repressed tendencies. That is the nature of projection, as we will explore later: making wrong over there what we cannot see or acknowledge over here. The more aware we become, and the more we accept all of who we are, the less we will be driven by unconscious and repressed forces, and the less likely we will fall prey to hubris.

## POWER IS SEDUCTIVE

Are we afraid that, like Gollum in *The Lord of the Rings,* we will be so seduced by power that we will lose all vestiges of ourselves, of our humanity?

There is no doubt that power is seductive, as are many of its trappings. Again, fame, money, and status are not intrinsically bad. Only when we become attached to them—when we lose ourselves or begin to sell out our beliefs, our convictions, our deepest natures in order to acquire, maintain, or expand them— are we at risk. The better we know ourselves and value who we are intrinsically, the less likely that we will depend on external, superficial, and transitory factors for validation and satisfaction.

With consciousness, mindfulness, and self-awareness we can have these things—and power—without being had by them.

## POWER CORRUPTS

*Power corrupts* are almost always the first words out of retreat participants' mouths when we begin the process of giving voice to negative beliefs about power. While there is truth to Lord Acton's invective, when read in context it seems to indicate that he was focusing on political power structures: "And remember, where you have a concentration of power in a few hands, all too frequently men with the mentality of gangsters get control. History has proven that. All power corrupts; absolute power corrupts absolutely." In other words, he wasn't talking about personal power, which is our focus here.

It is also true, as science fiction writer David Brin points out, that "power corrupts, but actually it's more true that power attracts the corruptible. The sane are usually attracted by other things than power." So, the question becomes how does Jesus, when tempted by power at the edge of the mountain top in the desert, or Frodo, the heroic ring bearer in *The Lord of the Rings*, resist the corrupting pull of power and not become enslaved by it?

How do we manage power with integrity, without selling ourselves out? How can we tell when we've crossed the line? It's tricky and can be a slippery slope. It's not hard to get hooked by power's seductive nature.

For me, it goes back to having a strong sense of self, which is only possible by knowing oneself deeply. Maybe we won't have an opportunity to prove our mettle on a heroic journey out in the world, from which we return to the community having gained wisdom and insight to share. But we all have access to—and I would further add, the call—to explore the Great Within, where wisdom is found. There, at the source, we

SELF-KNOWLEDGE AND SELF-AWARENESS ARE THE AMULETS PROTECTING US AGAINST THE SEDUCTIVE AND CORRUPTING FORCES OF POWER.

find self-acceptance and self-love. We naturally become a congruent expression of who we are. We connect with our empowered, soulful hero within. The more authentically powerful we feel, the less need there is to overcompensate with the strategies and games of worldly power. The call for heroism is universal, now more than ever!

And there are exemplars. Jimmy Carter stands out as someone who seems to have been able to handle power without getting corrupted by it, someone who grew as a person and in stature post-presidency. Similarly, Ellen DeGeneres, who walked away from a lucrative *American Idol* contract because it was not a match for her essence as a human being, seems to be able to manage the trappings of power without losing herself. She is refreshingly funny without being mean-spirited or making fun at others' expense.

Later we will consider some practices to help us with that. But first, let's look at some other ways we can learn to discern the difference between the types of power.

## POWER PRACTICES

Give some thought to and journal about the following questions:

- What holds you back from stepping fully into your power? (What people, situations, beliefs might be affected or change by your stepping into your power?)

- What scares you about power? (What might happen if you really stepped into your power?)

# PART IV

## DECONSTRUCTING OUR RELATIONSHIP TO POWER

# CHAPTER 15
## WE MUST CULTIVATE OUR GARDEN

How do we discern the difference between the types of power? And how do we then step into a healthy, soulful expression of power, one that is congruent with our essential nature? How do heroes and soulful leaders awaken the soul of power?

### DO YOUR HOMEWORK!

First, we must do our homework or, to adapt Voltaire's words, cultivate our own gardens. We must be willing to delve deep within and do the requisite work to allow unhealed areas to be healed, through whichever methods and modalities we are drawn to: therapy, breathwork, bodywork, spiritual coaching. We offer ourselves to and dive into the heroic quest of self-healing, the most honorable thing we can do, in my opinion. In so doing we become clear channels of soulful power, minimizing the chances that it will get tainted by our own egoic needs and result in abuse or overcompensation.

Speaking of breathwork, I'd like to give you a better idea of how powerful this process is. Having offered and facilitated this process now for more than three decades, I have yet to come across anything that heals as profoundly, as quickly and on as many levels as it does. It is the constant at every retreat or workshop I offer, in conjunction with the ego teachings. Those two make a powerful combination. While we dive deep within and do the heroic work of noticing and busting ourselves on our ego tendencies, even more healing happens in the breathwork. Countless times I have witnessed people heal traumatic experiences from childhood and beyond, which had subconsciously impacted their behavior, choices, and relationships for a lifetime. Many of us—and I would venture, most—were told or misheard things at an early age that have colored and impacted our lives. Or perhaps we misinterpreted situations from our limited capacity and perspective then—only to carry those notions with us for a lifetime.

Laurie, for example, remembers hearing her parents arguing about who was going to take her to soccer practice when she was probably five or six. A short time later they separated. Little Laurie, who did not know any better, made the assumption that it was her fault, and also internalized and personalized her father's leaving: "How could he leave me? What's wrong with me? Didn't he love me enough?" That assumption and misunderstanding had infused and distorted every relationship she'd ever had with a man. Because she did not value herself, she attracted men who were not her peers. During a retreat, she came to understand the pattern conceptually, and then during a breathwork session, she had a flash of the original memory, which allowed her to release the old belief that she was "not enough." No longer was she willing to sell out on her power or settle for less. Within a few months she met a guy who was a match for her, intellectually, emotionally, professionally, and in terms of shared values.

Cultivating our own gardens is a necessity and an ongoing process. Soulful power is about authentic self-expression. Implicit to that is valuing ourselves. A strong sense of self-worth is indispensable, and to attain that we must go within and do our work. As Roman philosopher Seneca wrote: "Most powerful is he who has himself in his own power."

On this journey it is crucial that we have companions who will help keep up honest—clear mirrors to keep us humble and real, who are just as committed to their own healing and to serving the world. In those clear mirrors we will see those blind spots in the back of our heads that we could not see otherwise.

What else stands in our way? What branches in our garden are blocking the light and are in need of pruning? What forms of fear have we allowed to hold us back—from following our dreams, from stepping into our fullness, from being fully open to joy, from fulfilling our potential?

## DECONSTRUCTING OUR RELATIONSHIP TO POWER

Deconstructing our relationship to power is part of cultivating our own garden. It entails understanding the difference between soulful and egoic power. It also involves identifying our own particular obstacles to power and power leaks. When and for what reasons do we resist it or refuse it or fear it? In what situations do we tend to give away our power?

The first step, which we have already begun to take, is identifying the beliefs and assumptions about power we have taken on from society and culture. This also includes analyzing the beliefs we have taken on about ourselves.

## BELIEFS ABOUT POWER

What are some commonly held fears or misconceptions about power?

- Power is not feminine.

- Power = Power over someone/something.

- Power corrupts.

- Power leads to abuse.

- Power alienates (generates fear or jealousy in others, a lack of acceptance, a loss of friends so we end up alone).

- All men are threatened by powerful women.

- Power disrupts and will bring about change to status quo. (Yes, when we step into our power things will change and that may feel scary, but the alternative—that another five, ten, twenty years will pass and we'll be stuck in the same limiting, soul-devouring and unfulfilling situations—is infinite scarier.)

- Good girls don't seek power. They are subservient and mind their own place.


## BELIEFS ABOUT SELF

While we are taking a look at our beliefs, let's extend that inventory to include our inner selves. What beliefs about ourselves have we outgrown and need to be pruned? Which misunderstandings are we ready to burn like a pile of leaves? No matter what negative beliefs we took on about ourselves—that we are stupid, ugly, a mess, a problem, unfit to be happy, unworthy of love—the answer is always the same: Bullshit!

Those negative beliefs are simply not true but misunderstandings of young minds that did not know any better. Perhaps someone said something to us the wrong way, not realizing the effect it would have on us. Maybe it was a coping mechanism, a way to protect ourselves from failure or abandonment. Whatever the origin, it was a confusion, a lie, a misconception, and it is never too late to correct. Cultivating our garden also means being mindful of messages we tell ourselves and involves the process of identifying and deleting negative and disempowering misunderstandings and untruths. Perhaps most importantly, it means identifying our own obstacles to love: What has kept me from fully accepting and loving myself and others? This too, is the work of heroes.

## POWER PRACTICE

- Make a list of negative or limiting beliefs about yourself. Don't judge, evaluate, or analyze it yet. It's all right if the items feel petty or superficial, as in "I'm too much of this, not enough of that." The process of compiling the list will be powerful enough. When you're finished, burn it.

# CHAPTER 16
## POWER PLAYS: THE DENIER

The second step in getting clear and resolving our ambivalence about power is fine-tuning our understanding about unhealthy (and often unconscious) power patterns. These are power plays that we have utilized as ways of coping and getting what we wanted. They got us somewhere, but they are not ultimately effective, and there is a price to pay for engaging them. These are among the pitfalls we encounter in the Zone of Power. We think these strategies are expressions of power, but they are mere decoys, illusions, and delusions of power.

Why would anyone want to suppress or deny their power? We'll look at this question more deeply a bit later but for now, suffice it to say that we become afraid of, confused by, or harbor misunderstandings about it. Women, in particular, can succumb to cultural conditioning and buy into the belief that they have to manage, diminish, or hide their power if they are to find a suitable mate. Though this is happening less and less as education and opportunity become more available and as patriarchal structures implode worldwide, too many women still take on the belief that they are merely meant to play supportive and nurturing roles as caregivers and reproductive machines. There is nothing inherently powerless about the roles of caregiving or mothering; in fact, they can certainly be enacted in powerful and even fierce ways. It is the buying into the cultural lies and conditioning that is the problem, the beliefs that keep women disempowered and playing small.

And it's no wonder! In addition to the general ambivalence toward power in our culture, for far too long now women have been taught—sometimes coerced by use of overpowering physical force—to stuff and stifle their power. It is still happening today, and for evidence we don't have to look to cultures where women have to cover their bodies or walk behind their men and cannot leave the house unaccompanied.

In 1988 in America, land of opportunity, where equality for all is ostensibly guaranteed by the Constitution and gradually becoming a reality, the Southern Baptist Convention, the largest Protestant denomination with close to 16 million members, added a section to their statement of faith, the Baptist Faith and Message, stating: "A wife is to submit herself graciously to the servant leadership of her husband even as the church willingly submits to the headship of Christ. She, being in the image of God as is her husband and thus equal to him, has the God-given responsibility to respect her husband and to serve as his helper in managing the household and nurturing the next generation."[9]

The denomination's decision in 2000 prohibiting women ministers prompted former president Jimmy Carter to break a family tradition and resign from the Southern Baptist Convention, citing an "increasingly rigid creed" and describing such interpretations as a "distortion of the meaning of Scripture."[10]

In the Roman Catholic Church, one of the most powerful strongholds of the patriarchy, Article 5 of the Congregation for the Doctrine of Faith (formerly known as the Supreme Sacred Congregation of the Roman and Universal Inquisition—yes, that Inquisition—led by Josef Cardinal Ratzinger until his advancement to Pope Benedict XVI), decreed as recently as July 2010 that "both the one who attempts to confer sacred ordination on a woman, and she who attempts to receive sacred ordination," will be excommunicated. Tellingly, this "grave crime" falls in the same category as pedophile priests.[11]

And still, women only make 77 cents to every dollar a man makes.

While there are complex historical and societal reasons for the gender power imbalance, the whys and hows are ultimately inconsequential.

Needless to say, women are not the only minorities experiencing oppression in the world today. Blacks, Latinos, immigrants, and LGBTQ people are among the disempowered, often excluded and discriminated against. I focus on women specifically here because misogyny connects to all other issues we face as a species.

Enough! Ain't nobody got any more time for that!

Let's take a deeper look at the patterns of power denying so that we can understand and deactivate them, because that's what heroes—of any gender, race, or sexual orientation—do.

## STRATEGIES POWER DENIERS USE TO RELINQUISH OR AVOID POWER

**Busyness.** We can easily avoid looking at ourselves by getting swept up into busyness. Not only that, but the adrenaline rush we sometimes get from nonstop activity—for example, juggling ten projects and a hectic schedule—can create a feeling of power, of being on top of things. Of course, the opposite is also true, and we can end up feeling out of control and overwhelmed. Either way we may be avoiding ourselves and our true power.

**False humility.** Humility does not mean self-denial, self-abasement, or putting oneself down. Unlike false humility—when we fear being perceived as prideful and then modify or downplay our attributes, experience, or accomplishments—humility is an internal state of being that is not concerned with what others think. Perhaps counterintuitively, it comes from an authentic place of power: who we are is simply who we are. Period. We require no one's validation and have no need to prove anything to anybody. Arrogance, on the other hand, usually stems from overconfidence and an inflated sense of self that mask deeper feelings of inadequacy and a need for external validation.

One of the problems with denying our power is that we know from physics that energy cannot be destroyed; it merely changes forms. Suppressed power has to come out somewhere, in some form. Frustrated and unexpressed power can turn into suppressed anger, which is then expressed inappropriately or else shows up in bodily symptoms such as heart attacks, ulcers, or cancer of the stomach, liver, or gallbladder.

> "TO CONFESS ONE HAS POWER IS TO MAKE ONESELF RESPONSIBLE FOR USING IT, AND SAFETY LIES IN AN ARTFULLY CONTRIVED POSE OF IMPOTENCE."
> —MICHAEL KORDA

It's the typical kick-the-dog syndrome. We sit back quietly while the boss is crude and unfair to us, swallow our real feelings, say "Yes, sir," or "Yes, ma'am," though we are seething inside. Then we walk away and take it out on others ranking lower on the hierarchy of power—subordinates, the spouse, the kids.

**Playing small.** I can't recall a single time at Women and Power retreats that someone *didn't* raise her hand when I asked how many had at some point minimized themselves or withheld some aspect of themselves out of concern of being seen as too fill-in-the-blank. Of course, men do that too, but the conditioning is different, and it happens less frequently. Ironically, playing small can be viewed as a type of arrogance. By acting as if we are something other than we are, we superimpose a false and smaller view of who we are and deny our true nature. How dare we, at this time when we are all needed to step up on behalf of humanity and our planet as we collectively choose between destruction and transformation? Marianne Williamson captures this beautifully in this quote from *A Return to Love*, which has gone around the world and even appeared in one of Nelson Mandela's speeches. It bears repeating:

Our deepest fear is not that we are inadequate. Our deepest fear is that we are powerful beyond measure. It is our light, not our darkness that most frightens us. We ask ourselves, Who am I to be brilliant, gorgeous, talented, fabulous? Actually, who are you not to be? You are a child of God. Your playing small does not serve the world. There is nothing enlightened about shrinking so that other people won't feel insecure around you. We are all meant to shine, as children do. We were born to make manifest the glory of God that is within us. It's not just in some of us; it's in everyone. And as we let our own light shine, we unconsciously give other people permission to do the same. As we are liberated from our own fear, our presence automatically liberates others.[12]

## POWER PRACTICE

- What is your payoff for not stepping into your power? (What do you get to do or not do as a result of denying your power?)

# CHAPTER 17

## POWER PLAYS:
## THE PSEUDO-MACHO

An overcompensation for deep and often subconscious feelings of powerlessness, this pattern manifests itself as a façade of bravado. We act like a "tough guy" on the outside, while inside we are barely keeping it together.

One problem with this particular strategy is that being inauthentic—putting on a show, acting as if we were something that we are not—takes a lot of work and uses up inordinate amounts of energy.

Another unintended negative consequence of the pseudo-macho tactic is that we can become hardened on the inside, frozen, or frigid. Suppressing emotions cannot be done selectively. When we suppress emotions such as fear, anger, or vulnerability, we end up suppressing others as well. Paraphrasing the words of Maia Dhyan, our ability to feel joy is contingent on our ability to feel sadness and pain. When we suppress anger or sadness, we also suppress joy—and end up with emotional numbness.

Hillary Clinton can be considered an example of the pseudo-macho. During the 2008 Democratic campaign at times she came across as ultra-hawkish, occasionally sounding like George W. Bush himself in her threats to go out and kick global butt. To be fair, she must have felt that being perceived as tough would be the only way she would be seen as a credible Commander in Chief and possibly get elected. After her tenure as U.S. Senator and Secretary of State, however, she seemed to drop into a more natural, relaxed, and authentic expression of herself and her power. Eight years later in the 2016 election cycle, she seemed much more comfortable in her skin and at ease in her leadership role. She even spoke about love in her speeches.

Interestingly, Obama in 2008 embodied much more the feminine principles of inclusiveness, dialogue, everyone at the table. People all across the world felt his authenticity and responded to that. I believe that's the reason people everywhere rallied behind him. He spoke to a part of us that has had enough with patriarchal, worldly, egoic power.

> "POWER IS LIKE BEING A LADY . . . IF YOU HAVE TO TELL PEOPLE YOU ARE, YOU AREN'T."
> —MARGARET THATCHER

## POWER PRACTICES

- Is there anyone in your life who employs the pseudo-macho tactic? Describe a recent incident in which someone you know used it. How did you feel afterward?

- Have you ever used the pseudo-macho technique? How did you feel afterward?

- On a scale of 1 to 10, how comfortable are you with your emotions? (1 = Um, what are emotions again? 10 = I'm fully able to feel and express them courageously, responsibly, and consistently, as needed.)

# Chapter 18
## POWER PLAYS: THE CRITIC (AKA THE JUDGE)

As we have already seen, judging is one of the ego's defining characteristics. Because we seldom keep our judgments to ourselves, the Judge manifests itself as the Critic. Criticizing others directly—whether alone or in the presence of others—can effectively put them "in their place" and disempower them. These power plays can often be evidenced in the workplace.

It is tragic to witness how often people who come to my retreats still nurse or cover up emotional wounds caused by hyper-critical parents. Often these parents' intention was a decent but misguided one of "toughening up" and readying their children for the world. Even so, the end results can still be harmful and long-lasting.

Confronting someone directly can be a source of fear and anxiety. To avoid anger and confrontation, we instead express our feelings in subtle, covert, and underhanded ways that are not effective. That unexpressed resentment builds up to the point it can no longer be stuffed, and it begins to dribble out in roundabout, indirect ways through veiled criticism, barbed remarks, sarcasm, and bitchy humor. The catty critic who masters bitchy humor that can almost makes its recipient bleed can be irresistibly funny, but this type of humor that depends on cutting down people is not only disempowering of others but ultimately to oneself. Putting someone else down—whether overtly or covertly—in order to feel good about ourselves, only generates a false and hollow sense of power, security, and well-being.

Ellen DeGeneres and Lily Tomlin are masters of the type of brilliant, incisive, and socially transformative humor that does not put others down. Admittedly, humor that makes fun of others can serve the purpose of defusing tense or highly charged situations when it is not used disrespectfully or mean-spiritedly and is administered equitably. That is a fine line to walk, though!

Gossip is another way to exert power unhealthily. It has less integrity than outright criticism because it is done behind another's back. Gossip is a tool of the powerless and can have harmful consequences, impact others' reputations, and destroy lives, friendships, and relationships. Diminishing another ultimately diminishes us. Though it might seem to boost our power standing momentarily, it is a cheap and dangerous way to gain status. Better to follow the adage, "If you have nothing positive to say about someone, it's better not to say anything." Asking ourselves, "How do I feel afterward?" will always yield valuable insight. We might derive momentary pleasure from gossiping but most often we end up feeling as though we need a shower.

If you have information about someone that could prevent another person from being harmed, that is important to share. If you are honestly trying to protect that person, you just need to be clean and honest and acknowledge if what you are telling them is hearsay. In addition, you can recommend they do their own research and check with their own feelings.

To author Erica Jong, "Gossip is the opiate of the oppressed." None other than Albert Einstein had this to say: "If A equals success, then the formula is A equals X plus Y and Z, with X being work, Y play, and Z keeping your mouth shut." Which reminds me of an old Cuban saying: "Vas a morir por la lengua, como el pescado," or "You will die like a fish because of your tongue." (The word *por* means both "through" and "because of" in this context.)

Two final words of wisdom on this topic: Rule #1 in Dale Carnegie's best-selling book *How to Make Friends and Influence People* is "Never criticize, condemn or complain." By now I trust you realize this does not mean stuffing our truth in order to be nice or avoid conflict. Whenever there are issues that need to be addressed in our relationships, we learn how to create healthy boundaries and communicate our feelings and needs courageously, powerfully, yet gracefully. And finally, there's this quote attributed to both the Quakers and Indian sage Shirdi Sai Baba. Before you speak, ask yourself: "Is it kind? Is it true? Is it necessary? Does it improve upon the silence?" Wise words for heroes.

> "IS IT KIND? IS IT TRUE? IS IT NECESSARY? DOES IT IMPROVE UPON THE SILENCE?"

## POWER PRACTICES

- When was the last time you gossiped or criticized people behind their back? How did you feel afterward? From your current vantage point, how else might you have handled the situation? Journal this.

- For one day this week, keep a tab in your journal of every time you notice the inner critic. Is this a familiar voice inside your head? Who does it remind you of? What patterns do you notice? Are there certain situations or people that tend to activate the inner critic?

# CHAPTER 19
## POWER PLAYS: THE ABUSER (AKA THE BULLY)

We can think of abusing power as going over to the dark side. Normally this stems from woundedness, revenge, greed, or overcompensation. A drastic example is Darth Vader, whose trajectory to the dark side we'll examine later. But there is no need to think of extremes like the Death Star blowing up an entire planet. We go over to the dark side every time we allow ourselves to become reactive, take revenge, say something hurtful to or about someone else, kick the dog, hit the wife or kids.

As noted earlier, the U.S. is a great example of abuse of power. The way we squandered the goodwill of the world after 9/11, misusing and corrupting our status as sole superpower, is nothing less than tragic. We should know by now that you can't put out a fire with gasoline. The rise of ISIS and the continued military involvement in Afghanistan and Iraq—with all its incalculable human and financial costs—are evidence of the effects of that action.

More often than not, bullies are cowardly and prone to bluffing. As Benjamin Disraeli said, "Courage is fire, and bullying is smoke." Bullies are intuitively good at identifying prey who are weaker than they are and who won't likely put up a challenge.

But when their bluff is called and they are confronted by those willing to take a stand for themselves, bullies will usually retreat.

We tend to think of abuse of power in the sense of brutal forcefulness; however, it is often experienced in other, sometimes nonphysical, ways. Examples include child sexual abuse; a boss who keeps his team walking on eggshells with the implicit fear of being fired; sexual improprieties between psychotherapists and their patients, or religious leaders and those to whom they minister; a bratty, self-deluded movie star who terrorizes a set or demolishes a hotel room.

Sadly, because of what it implies about human nature, kids can be incredibly cruel to each other. Consider cyberbullying, which has been responsible for several incidents of teen suicide. About 42 percent of youths have experienced cyberbullying and 5 percent have felt fear about their safety.[13] One of the factors accounting for the prevalence—and danger—of cyberbullying is it can provide anonymity for the perpetrator. And because it uses emotional and psychological attack rather than the brute force more typically experienced on the school playground, cyberbullying involves more female participation.

At one point in high school I experienced a short stint as a bully. I participated in making fun of this one student on whom everybody picked. I confess this because it might shed light on what can motivate bullying. As mentioned earlier, I was a newcomer and an outsider in high school, and for the first year and a half did not have friends or belong to any group. In 10th grade I befriended a few guys who, for some reason, spent a semester ostracizing this one student in funny ways—to everyone else, but obviously not to the student. My only really active involvement, my pièce de résistance, was a poem inspired by the name he had been given because of his eating propensities at break and lunch. The poem, Ode to Meatpie, flowed out of me on the bus ride home one afternoon with disturbing ease and was circulated surreptitiously during class the next day. Sadly, although I had felt marginalized myself, I took part in helping to marginalize this other person. In some twisted way, it made me more accepted and my coolness status went up.

Besides boosting my peer acceptance level, I suspect a deeper, subconscious dynamic: the desire to deflect attention from myself and my deep struggle with being gay. It is interesting and telling that three of us in this group eventually turned out to be gay. Of course, I don't believe that being gay causes bullying. At work here were the mechanisms of displacement and scapegoating. This example also provides a commentary on a society that makes an intrinsic part of being human so wrong that the oppressed become the oppressors. As a society, when the word *gay* is used as an epithet and a weapon, and embodies all that could be insulting and derogatory to teenagers and even preteens, we need to look at the consequences that may engender. In this case the self-hatred and internal conflict we felt about ourselves and our tenuous social status in school found an avenue and all that anguish, confusion, frustration, fear, and anger got projected onto a weaker member of the class.

> "ANYONE ENTRUSTED WITH POWER WILL ABUSE IT IF NOT ALSO ANIMATED WITH THE LOVE OF TRUTH AND VIRTUE, NO MATTER WHETHER HE BE A PRINCE, OR ONE OF THE PEOPLE."
> —JEAN DE LA FONTAINE

From my current vantage point, I can see that the ingratiating ways that made this student challenging to be with were only a symptom of his own lack of identity and self-love. Though I was not one of the worst offenders by any stretch of the imagination, I certainly caused harm to this person. For that, I am profoundly sorry.

## POWER PRACTICES

- Have there been situations in your past in which you participated in bullying others? From current perspective, what underlying dynamics were at play with you?

- In what ways is your ego—your inner critic—still bullying you?

- If you were bullied yourself, I am deeply sorry you had that experience. No one, especially young persons, should have to go through that. Have you done any healing work around that? Does the story above help provide perspective or understanding?

# CHAPTER 20
## POWER PLAYS: THE AVENGER

Revenge is a hollow victory and fails to deliver what we really want—a sense of reclaiming power that we feel (rightly or wrongly) has been taken from us. When we seek revenge, we are attempting to bring balance and right a perceived wrong.

Yet, as many of us have learned, the resulting feeling of satisfaction is short-lived and empty, and often the situation is not even corrected. Worse yet, we have failed to bring resolution to the conflict and have most likely made it worse.

How many more ways do we need to hear it? "Two wrongs don't make a right." "Violence begets violence." Or in Gandhi's words: "An eye for an eye makes the whole world go blind." When we undertake revenge at the personal level, we lessen, cheapen, and endanger ourselves. At the international level, we undermine our future.

Although it may seem counterintuitive, there is more power in, as Jesus taught, "turning the other cheek." A scene in the film *Gandhi* depicts the famous Salt March, during which the spiritual leader leads thousands of Indians almost 250 miles to the sea to collect salt in a symbolic act of civil disobedience and in protest of an exorbitant and unfair tax. When their path is temporarily blocked by British military, the Indians, with fear and determination in their faces, proceed up to the gate where they inevitably get struck down by the soldiers. Watching that scene, as harrowing as it is, one can feel with every blow the will and the power of the British Empire waning—and India's rising.

*Satyagraha*, Gandhi's concept of nonviolence, derives from the Sanskrit words *satya* for "truth" and *graha*, "holding firm on to," which he also translated as "love force or soul-force." We can also think of it as soulful power.

Needless to say, we are not talking here about becoming a doormat or allowing others to take advantage of us. We are making a conscious choice. There is a time to confront, and we can learn to do that gracefully without diminishing ourselves or abusing others, in a way that can be heard and received, not deflected, defended against, or denied. And certainly, without generating a reaction that will continue to fuel the endless cycle of violence and revenge—whether physical, emotional, or spiritual.

One of the problems with revenge is that it keeps us stuck in the situation, ruminating about it, feeling angry or victimized, plotting our retribution. As long as we keep ourselves in that prison, we perpetuate our own suffering and keep our own wounds festering. We are unable to move beyond the situation. Peace and healing remain unattainable.

In the iconic film series *Star Wars*, which George Lucas based on the hero's journey, Anakin Skywalker turns to the dark side—and succumbs to out-of-control worldly power—when he gives in to feelings of revenge. Enraged when he arrives too late to rescue his mother, he abuses his Jedi powers and massacres the raiders who had enslaved her.

Two other things to ponder regarding this subject: One, "There is no revenge so complete as forgiveness," said Josh Billings, the 19th century humorist and writer. We will focus on this quality—an aspect of soulful power—later. And two, in the words of Francis Bacon, the 16th century scientist and philosopher: "In taking revenge, a man is but even with his enemy; but in passing it over, he is superior." In overriding the reactive desire for revenge, we set ourselves free.

HEROES CHOOSE TO GET FREE, NOT EVEN.

## POWER PRACTICE

- Think of a situation in which you took revenge on someone, even subtly, such as gossiping or twisting the truth about them. How did you feel afterward? What effects did your behavior generate?

# CHAPTER 21
## POWER PLAYS: THE BITCH/ BASTARD

Most of us have been mauled by a bitch or screwed over by a bastard. And we all—regardless of gender—have an inner bitch that can rear its head under pressure. More than the regrettable occasional slipup, the concern here is when the behavior becomes a pattern.

Whereas the Bully is usually more direct, in-your-face, and blatant, the Bitch can be more subtle, conniving, and manipulative, creating conflict and wreaking havoc behind the scenes, pitting one against the other, acting nice and friendly while sticking a knife in your back. The Bitch and the Bastard are opportunists and can turn on a dime. Out for themselves, they can be friend today, foe tomorrow.

Joan Crawford, as portrayed in the film *Mommie Dearest,* is an example, as are Aubrey, the leader of the Bellas, in the film *Pitch Perfect;* Alexis in the TV series *Dynasty*; and both Frank and Claire Underwood in *House of Cards*.

This pattern probably develops from overcompensation for past woundedness or perceived powerlessness, and like the others, it offers transitory and hollow satisfaction. It seldom, if ever, engenders what we—social animals that we are, after all—truly want: love, respect, friendship, a sense of belonging, feelings of empowerment, community. Heroes learn to avoid the Bitch

Trap and the Bastard Pitfall, both decoys and expressions of pseudo-power.

A note on the Bitch and leadership style: evidence of misogyny is not hard to find in our society. The very same qualities that in a man evoke admiration and are considered strong leadership qualities—decisiveness, directiveness, clarity in communication, speaking out first, the willingness to communicate one's preferences, boundaries or needs—in a woman can be reduced to and interpreted as symptoms of being a bitch.

> BUT THUS DO I COUNSEL YOU, MY FRIENDS: DISTRUST ALL IN WHOM THE IMPULSE TO PUNISH IS POWERFUL!"
> —FRIEDRICH NIETZSCHE

## POWER PRACTICES

- Think of a situation in which you unleashed your inner bitch on someone. How did you feel afterward? What effects did your behavior have on the person involved and on your relationship with them?

- Which bitch characters do you love to hate? What qualities do you appreciate in them? Which do you reject?

# CHAPTER 22
## POWER PLAYS: THE RESISTER

Resisting is a way of rebelling, an attempt to unhealthily and indirectly assert our power, though not very gracefully or, in the long term, effectively. On the outside we may be saying "Yes, dear," while internally, perhaps even subconsciously, we are thinking: "Screw you; I'll do it when I'm good and ready. I'll show you who has the real power here."

This pattern of behavior often reveals itself in the workplace, by sabotaging projects, for example, or dragging our feet, slowing down production. We may be saying "yes" but our actions reveal "no."

In personal relationships, withholding sex can be an expression of passive-aggressiveness—an even more complex form of resistance. We may say "Sorry, honey, I have a headache," but our internal dialogue may be more like: "Hell will freeze over before you get any tonight!" As poet and playwright Oscar Wilde quipped with his inimitable wit and piercing perspective into human nature: "Everything in the world is about sex except sex. Sex is about power."

What's the downside? How does passive-aggressiveness harm us? Even though this behavior is often subconscious, saying one thing and being another generates internal conflict and requires high levels of psychic energy expenditure. We deny—even to ourselves—that we are acting out in a rebellious or resistant manner. Ultimately, it is neither empowering nor satisfying.

Though this, like other power games, might bring about some immediate pleasure, such as driving another to the point of exasperation and losing their cool, that feeling is temporary and does not provide the relief that an authentic expression of personal power brings about. Even to ourselves, if we are honest, it feels sneaky, subterranean, and lame. At some level we know we are weaseling out of a confrontation.

There is such freedom—and power—in just being ourselves and simply saying what works for us and what does not!

## POWER PRACTICES

- Identify someone in your life who tends to use passive-aggressive behavior as a power play. How effective a strategy is it? Do they often achieve their goal or get what they want? At what price? What is the impact on their relationship with you and with others?

- Think of a time in which you may have slipped into passive-aggressive behavior. From your current perspective, how might you handle the situation differently today?

# CHAPTER 23
## POWER PLAYS: THE VICTIM

Renouncing the Victim is the single most important act of empowerment we can take. It is not easy, as the victim dynamic is subtle and insidious and has been inculcated into our consciousness. It is nothing less than an act of heroism.

When presenting the ego in my retreats, this is the most challenging part for many people to navigate. Like Janice, who for years had been in an adversarial relationship with her ex-husband, whom she blamed for many things, including the fact she felt stuck carrying the heavy financial weight of a house they both still owned and had been trying to unload for years. I told her that the house situation would resolve itself once she healed the relationship with the ex. She fought me all weekend. She'd built an almost airtight case as to why she was in the right, and how he had wronged and hurt her. I kept repeating that it wasn't about him and that there was no excuse for what he did or didn't do, but if she wanted to be free, she needed to forgive him and let go of her anger. Finally, on the last breathwork session on Sunday, she had a vision of herself as an angel gently flying down from above him as he slept and kissing him on the forehead. Forgiveness had happened. On Monday, the house sold. (I kid you not. And I'm not exaggerating. This stuff really works!)

Similarly, Linda was holding on to feeling outraged at her ex-husband for all the things he had done and failed to do. She also fought me all weekend and said she would never forgive him. In her case it took several years, but she eventually reached out and told me she was finally able to do it and was now in a great new relationship. Which is what I'd told her—that she had to clean up and clear out the old before the new could come in.

Others who have attended my retreats and received the ego teachings are still living in victim mode. Benjamin slips in and out of blaming his prejudiced former employers, his health condition, the unfair healthcare system, the uncaring government for his, to be sure, unenviable situation. Regardless of the merit of his contentions though, Benjamin needs to do his inner work before things will change for him. While I have deep empathy and compassion for everyone dealing with painful problems, I often witness firsthand how we remain victims—imprisoned and disempowered—as long as we hold someone or something external to us responsible for our way of being.

I know this is hard stuff. I don't use the word heroic lightly! Without a doubt, the discussion about the Victim is what has elicited the most pushback in retreats over the years. It's the least favorite part of my job—struggling with someone who is stuck in victim mode. What is difficult for them to see in the moment is that I am actually advocating on their behalf, taking a stand for their freedom, and trying to maintain an open heart even when I am being opposed or even attacked. I realize it's not personal and know that the ego has a deep attachment to the status quo, even when it's miserable. Popping out of victim mode is nothing short of heroic, as is forgiving the unforgivable for the sake of our freedom. Again, it's not about *them*, and it certainly doesn't make what they did alright. It's about our freedom.

Playing the victim works; otherwise we would not do it. It can be an effective yet self-defeating way to get sympathy or attention: "Poor me. Woe is me! Look what my mother/father/spouse/teacher/minister/the world has done to me!" As an expression of pseudo-power, it can also be used to get others to do what we want, and in this sense can be a way to gain or maintain control over others.

At what price, though, do we engage the Victim? This strategy is antithetical to authentic power. As long as we keep placing blame or responsibility on others, we sacrifice our own power.

With power comes responsibility. "Wait. What was that? Responsibility?" Yep, that's right. Responsibility is unavoidable on the path to empowerment. If you're not up for it, I understand, but you might as well close this book right now and give it to a friend.

Why would we want to give our power away? Why is it more comfortable to have someone else be responsible?

Now we arrive at the greatest payoff of victimhood, which is that we get to hide, disappear, play small, lick our wounds in a corner feeling bad for ourselves. We keep ourselves safe (we think) from the possibility of failing. However, the rub is we also keep away the possibility of succeeding, thereby ensuring failure. The bottom line is that we get to shirk off responsibility. It is much easier to look the other away, to place responsibility for our failures or situation on others. "Oh, well, got a tough break this time round—bad genes, incapable parents, a bad upbringing, health problems . . ." The list of possible excuses is endless. As long as we are looking outside ourselves for the cause of our problems, we remain stuck in self-made prisons of victimhood. Self-made because we always have a choice as to how we show up in response to life's inevitable curve balls.

> AS LONG AS WE ARE LOOKING OUTSIDE OURSELVES FOR THE CAUSE OF OUR PROBLEMS, WE REMAIN STUCK IN SELF-MADE PRISONS OF VICTIMHOOD.

Let's take a closer look at that word *responsibility*. My former teacher Maia Dhyan taught that by splitting the word we get *response* and *ability*—the ability to respond. How do I choose to be in response to this situation? I would take it a step further. As we will explore more deeply later, the word *power* comes from the Latin root meaning "to be able to." We can therefore think of responsibility as "the power to respond."

Granted, taking responsibility for our lives and for our actions is not easy. In the final analysis, we are talking about nothing less than an evolutionary leap in consciousness.

Some spiritual teachings say that at a soul level we choose the circumstances of our lives—our families, place of birth, everything that happens to us, even illness and catastrophic events. While I can accept that theoretically, and can see the potential for learning and growth by giving ourselves challenges, I don't know with certainty that this is the way "the system" is set up. What I do have zero doubt about, however, is that no matter what curveballs life throws our way, we can *always* choose how we are going to be and how we will respond to any circumstance.

I feel fortunate that as a senior in high school my Advanced Placement Psychology professor took our class to hear Austrian psychiatrist Viktor Frankl speak. True to his vocation, during his years in concentration camps Frankl pondered why some people survived and others did not. He arrived at the conclusion that survival had nothing to do with intelligence, strength, body size, looks, social class, education, or the like. Rather, it was those who had a sense of meaning who found the will to survive. Significantly, Frankl realized that having a sense of meaning enabled one to choose one's response to any situation in life. That is why getting clear about our purpose is so critical, and why we delve into that more deeply in the Soulful Purpose retreats and Book 3 in the *Calling All Heroes* series.

As Frankl writes in *Man's Search for Meaning,* "We who lived in concentration camps can remember the men who walked through the huts comforting others, giving away their last piece of bread. They may have been few in number, but they offer sufficient proof that everything can be taken from a man but one thing: the last of the human freedoms—to choose one's attitude in any given set of circumstances, to choose one's own way."[14]

Assuming responsibility for our lives, relinquishing the Victim, does not involve denying or ignoring our past or exonerating anyone's behavior or their abuses of power. But it does mean letting go of our feelings of victimization, of having been "done to." We stop focusing on that, giving our power away to that. Basically, we are shelving the old, tired life script and creating a new context for our lives: "OK, so that happened, and it sucked. I wish things had been different. Life may have been easier (though, who knows?) without all that. The question is what am I going to do now? Whether I chose this at a soul level or not, at least I can choose now how I will respond to the situation. How will I choose to be in this moment, in spite of everything that happened or failed to happen in the past? That choice no one can take away from me. Not anymore. I am committed to going for it, to being the most that I can be, now and forever more, no matter what."

Blaming others—the world, life, God, the prevailing power structure, the patriarchy, slavery, our parents, the unfair boss, or the pederast priest—keeps us hopelessly trapped in powerlessness, stuck in victim consciousness. Which is very unpleasant, unfulfilling, and unattractive! Instead, we no longer succumb or give in to that tendency, or allow that pattern in ourselves. We must lay to rest "Poor me. Woe is me." It no longer serves us. We must stop blaming others. Now. Period. Next. If you are still reading this, it is time to banish the inner victim.

Claiming choice is always and inevitably empowering. Realizing that the universe is not out to get us, we become the architects of our lives, and everything begins to change. When we stop having an adversarial or victim/perpetrator relationship with any aspect of life, we open up to unexpected miracles and synchronicities. Things start coming together unexpectedly as if by magic or design. When we let go of victim mentality and start living this way, even the poor ego begins to be freed from its tired repertoire of behavior and feelings. What freedom! What a relief!

> "BETWEEN STIMULUS AND RESPONSE, THERE IS A SPACE. IN THAT SPACE IS OUR POWER TO CHOOSE OUR RESPONSE. IN OUR RESPONSE LIES OUR GROWTH AND OUR FREEDOM."
> —VIKTOR FRANKL

That's the heroic path.

## POWER PRACTICES

- Identify someone in your life who tends to play the Victim as a power play. How effective is this strategy? Do they often achieve their goal or get what they want? At what price? What is the impact on their relationship with you and with others?

- Think of a time in which you may have slipped into victim behavior. From your current perspective, how might you handle the situation differently today?

# Chapter 24

## Outgrowing Power Plays

To a certain degree these power plays, these survival techniques, have helped us get by and gotten us this far. This is true for most behavior patterns no matter how unhealthy. They were developed as coping mechanisms at an early age when we could not come up with a better way to cope. Rather than making them wrong, we need to realize that we no longer need the type of protection they have provided. We are much stronger than we think. We have proven to ourselves that we have survived—otherwise we would not still be here—and we can now leave behind these behavior patterns, like a snake skin we have outgrown, as we learn more efficient ways of being.

And if a high-values, moral stance does not inspire you sufficiently to avoid these unhealthy power patterns, remember this: What goes around usually comes around. That is to say, we are taking the high road because it is the right thing to do and because we are choosing to embrace a "Do no harm" personal moral policy. In other words, we are committing to not abuse or misuse power. If that is not enough of a motivator, then perhaps this will help: Sooner or later, Karma Cop will come for us!

We have begun deconstructing our beliefs about power, discussed the importance of cultivating our own gardens, and looked at some unhealthy patterns or stereotypes of power.

In some important ways and for reasons outlined at the beginning of this book, I have given particularly emphasis in the pages to the empowerment of women. Yet, we can't ignore the other half of the equation if we seek to bring healing and balance to our world. In the next chapter we explore what it means to be a man in the 21st century.

## POWER PRACTICES

- When do you feel least powerful?
- When do you feel most powerful?

# CHAPTER 25
## UPGRADING TO A NEW VERSION OF MASCULINITY

W e're all guilty of power plays but it's clear that women have paid a steep price in terms of oppressive rules, abusive treatment, and lack of opportunity—including not being free to fully express themselves and explore all options life offers. But what about men? The patriarchal system has crippled their options and opportunities as well.

The American Psychological Association recently tweeted: "Research shows that boys and men are at a disproportionate risk for school discipline, academic challenges, health disparities, and other quality of life issues."[15] And according to the National Institute for Mental Health, the suicide rate among males is almost four times as high as females.[16]

Why? Henry Rollins tries to answer that question in the *Los Angeles Times*: "By age 13, I was, and still am, a workaholic. From then to now, it's not about the money and it's beyond self-sufficiency. It's what I think a 'real man' must do. I am unable to shake myself of this, but at least I know where I got it from. . . . These standards—and postures many American males contort themselves to—are not without consequence. Beyond misplaced anger, feelings of inadequacy and hopelessness, the men who hold their emotions in check—like a stress position used to induce confession—sometimes break. White American males—mostly middle-age—accounted for 70 percent of suicides in 2017."[17]

What's going on? Is it possible that as a result of the intolerable and reprehensible oppression women have experienced for the last several thousand years, men have paid an equally steep price for their dominance by unwittingly creating a self-made prison? Are they now experiencing long-term repercussions from this kind of toxic masculinity? Does the patriarchy disempower men—in different ways?

In designating women and the feminine as inferior, men have limited their own range of behavior and human experience. The conditioning starts from an early age: "I'm gonna toughen you up, boy!" "Boys don't cry." "You throw like a girl." "Man up and grow some balls!"

If you're a "real man," you cannot wear certain colors, make certain hand movements, or cross your legs a certain way. In the playground when I was growing up, crossing your fingers this way or another—I don't recall which—meant you were girly. It meant you were less than a man.

Misogyny training, which starts at an early age, can be subtle and insidious. Some years ago, when "Governator" Arnold Schwarzenegger called Democratic opponents "girly men," Californians predictably complained and protested his disrespectful language. However, the underlying premise—that girliness is a bad thing and can therefore be used as an insult—was mostly overlooked. And therein lies the problem!

Up until recent times, most humans—especially men—have grown up with the internalized belief that it's not OK to feel emotions because that's a sign of weakness. Anger, perhaps, is the exception, but that is still seen as loss of control, and having everything under control is a manly goal. Feelings were downgraded and relegated to the realm of the feminine, which was considered lesser and subordinate. Emotions were ignored, suppressed, and exiled. The result? Inappropriate and reactive expressions of emotions. Rage (a build-up of suppressed anger). Depression (congealed, unexpressed grief). Health problems:

ulcers, cancer, and heart attacks. There is also a heavy price to be paid in unhealthy relationships, high levels of divorce, and lack of intimacy. Who wants to be in relationship with a robotic, unfeeling, undemonstrative zombie?

In his book *The Man They Wanted Me to Be*, Jared Yates Sexton writes about how his troublesome relationship with his father finally began to change as the latter approached the end of his life. "But what was most amazing, other than my father's apparent transformation, was that Dad, seemingly exhausted by years of near-silence, began to speak openly about the burden of masculinity. He told me the expectations he'd carried, as a father, as a son, as a man, had sabotaged his relationships and prevented him from expressing himself, or really enjoying intimacy, emotionally or intellectually, his entire life.... Traditional masculinity, as we know it, is an unnatural state, and, as a consequence, men are constantly at war with themselves and the world around them."[18]

And if health problems, longevity issues and higher suicide rates were not bad enough, men are falling behind in terms of education and workplace opportunities. As we continue to evolve as a species and more women emancipate themselves from the shackles imposed by an anachronistic patriarchal system that is no longer sustainable, the less dependent they become on their male counterparts. In the U.S., the number of women college graduates has surpassed men. In 2018, among women, 36 percent had earned a college degree by age 31, while only 28 percent of men had met that goal. And in 2015, according to the Bureau of Statistics, in 38 percent of heterosexual marriages in the U.S., the woman earned more than her male counterpart. That is a dramatic change from 1987, when that number was less than 25 percent.[19]

As women reclaim their power, they increasingly want it all—and should be able to have it. In bed many want to be pleasured, respected, honored, and sometimes ravished. In life they want an equal partner, not only generous in bed, but responsible, responsive, respectful, communicative, self-aware, fun, funny, intelligent, sensitive, and interested in more than cars, guns, and sports.

That's quite a tall order to fill! No wonder men are feeling threatened, confused, and left out as the power dynamics shift. As society has changed and women become empowered and reject old ways of being, many men find themselves mystified by the changing rules and expectations of what it means to be a man. In some cases, that confusion and the subconscious or unexpressed fear of not being able to meet the mark turns into anger and gets projected at women.

According to data compiled by the Giffords Law Center, in the U.S. 600 women are shot to death annually by intimate partners.[20] Moreover, a 2019 *Mother Jones* exposé on mass shootings revealed some disturbing patterns and connections to toxic masculinity. Of the 22 mass shooters studied—all men—86 percent had a history of domestic abuse; 50 percent specifically targeted women; and 32 percent had a history of stalking and harassment. Two of the perpetrators were considered "incels"—a mostly online subculture of "virulent misogynists who self-identify as 'involuntarily celibate' and voice their rage and revenge fantasies against women online."[21]

Houston, we've got a problem. We need an updated version of masculinity.

## RESET! MASCULINITY NEEDS AN UPDATE

What makes a man anyway? Surely more than a penis, balls, a Y chromosome, and extra testosterone. Is it the fuck-or-kill mentality? The swagger, the sense of entitlement, the ability to beat another into a pulp? Being able to throw a football and enjoy inflicting pain on others? How big a gun they pack? Is that what Rush Limbaugh meant by referring to Donald Trump as "Mr. Man" in his comments about then-presidential candidate Pete Buttigieg: "OK, how's this going to look, a 37-year-old gay guy kissing his husband onstage next to Mr. Man Donald Trump?" What exactly makes Trump a "real man?" Is it because he is offensive, rude, a bully? Because he insults people and abuses power? Or perhaps because he is rich and famous, has multiple affairs with women while married, pays off porn stars and grabs women by their private parts?

Really? Give me a break. What a petty, simplistic, superficial, and limiting way to define manhood. How confused we are! The truth is that most men are scared . . . to feel, to let go, to surrender. They are ruled by the false belief that feeling and expressing are less than masculine, signs of weakness. And understandably, many worry about not being good enough and fear they are not passing muster in this new world of ours.

These days it's a new game altogether. The transgender movement is forcing all of us to redefine and expand our concepts of gender. We have even witnessed a (not fully transitioned) man get pregnant!

We need a re-envisioned masculinity. It's time to evolve. Caveman mentality has been ruling the world far too long, and if we don't do something about it soon, well, we're going to be in much bigger trouble as a species. We need a real Men's Liberation—from the self-imposed prison—so we can limit the expression and experience of toxic masculinity for everyone.

So, what then does it mean to be a man in the 21st century? There remain plenty of opportunities to establish one's manhood in our changing times. Here are some traditional male roles re-envisioned, redefined, upgraded, and updated.

## The Provider

The statistics above point to one reason many men are struggling. Not only is technology replacing many of the jobs men used to perform, but women are starting to earn more money. In many households, men can no longer identify as the main breadwinner. So much for man as provider. I don't mean to come across as glib. My heart goes out to men of older generations for whom providing for their families was a core identity. To see industries collapse and jobs taken over by machines or outsourced to other countries with cheaper labor has to be difficult, to say the least. Finding oneself suddenly depending on others or having to receive government assistance after a lifetime of hard work has to be profoundly painful. As a result, many men surely internalize that as a personal failure and feel shame, humiliation, and a lack of purpose.

It doesn't have to be that way; men don't have to give up the provider identity, just expand it. There is so much you can still provide as a man, including a safe psychological and emotional space in which your spouse and family can thrive, discover who they are, and live to their fullest. You can provide stability and become a rock in the family structure, sharing the wisdom and strength that comes from self-knowledge and the willingness to do the work of self-healing. By providing unconditional love, support, and frequent praise and allowing room for mistakes and imperfection, you can help create a space in which self-love and self-acceptance thrive. There is no greater gift you can give your loved ones. You can also provide for your family an example of living with honesty, integrity, and other high values.

And wouldn't it be powerful and affirming to know that your spouse may not be dependent on you financially and still choose you freely—from a place of love, not need?

*The Protector*

In our increasingly complex world, there are many things outside our control, from which we can offer no protection. However, you can still protect your loved ones to the best of your capacity by imparting wisdom and experience. By teaching self-love, self-respect, and self-awareness, you are preparing them to face whatever challenges come their way. You can help protect them by modeling a different way of living heroically, and by making sure they always feel seen, valued, and respected.

You can help protect the poor, the weak, and the disenfranchised. Protect the young: Become a Big Brother or mentor. Coach a Little League team. Protect animals. Serve as a sacred steward of the Earth. We can sure use more ecologically minded, creative entrepreneurs to defend and protect the planet right about now!

In his book *The Hidden Spirituality of Men: Ten Metaphors to Awaken the Sacred Masculine*, Matthew Fox recommends invoking the Green Man archetype for inspiration—a custodian of the land who personifies soulful power, a strength that is both powerful and caring.[22]

In this era of disinformation and "alternative facts," protect the truth as you see it. That requires staying alert, informed, and doing your own research and due diligence, especially on social media. Champion the values in which you believe, especially by example. Get involved. Act. Act up when necessary.

Draw on the Servant King archetype. You may not have a kingdom to rule, but your home is your realm. Create for your family a sanctuary from fear, hatred, and negativity. Protect your employees or team members from negative competition and mediocrity. Encourage them to go for their personal best. Create an environment that supports personal and professional growth, one in which they can thrive as people, not just employees. Declare your home and your workplace universal peace zones, places where inner peace is valued and actively encouraged.

Protect yourself from exhaustion and burnout, from cynicism, indifference, and negative thinking. Protect your mind as well from meaninglessness, emotional repression, and unhealthy behaviors. To do that you must walk your talk. Go within and know yourself. You won't be able to do this while channel surfing on the couch.

"A MAN DIES WHEN HE REFUSES TO STAND UP FOR THAT WHICH IS RIGHT. A MAN DIES WHEN HE REFUSES TO STAND UP FOR JUSTICE. A MAN DIES WHEN HE REFUSES TO TAKE A STAND FOR THAT WHICH IS TRUE."
—MARTIN LUTHER KING, JR.

## The Hunter

Related to the provider, the hunter is a role that men have played from ancient times. In these times of 24-hour grocery stores, corner bodegas, Amazon, Grubhub, and HelloFresh, hunters are no longer in high demand in the developed world. Instead, how about hunting for solutions to the many problems we face as a species—war, poverty, terrorism, income inequality, hunger, hatred, xenophobia, immigration, polarization, the environmental crisis? Hunt down your own inner obstacles to growth. You will feel much stronger, freer, and happier. In the process, you will be of deep service to your family and beyond.

> "WE ARE NOT CONSUMERS. FOR MOST OF HUMANITY'S EXISTENCE, WE WERE MAKERS, NOT CONSUMERS: WE MADE OUR CLOTHES, SHELTER, AND EDUCATION, WE HUNTED AND GATHERED OUR FOOD.... WE ARE NOT ADDICTS. I PROPOSE THAT MOST ADDICTIONS COME FROM OUR SURRENDERING OUR REAL POWERS, THAT IS, OUR POWERS OF CREATIVITY."
> —MATTHEW FOX

## The Conqueror

We desperately need healthier conqueror energy in the world. Apply that energy to the inner conquest—the ultimate frontier. Conquer the ego's lower tendencies. Conquer your own inner demons.

Conquer your own fears and obstacles to love. "Conquering" a woman is much more than getting into her pants or deflowering her. Come on. What does that prove? What if instead you took on conquering her fear of or resistance to love?

To be able to do that you must first:

- Know yourself deeply.

- Become accountable and trustworthy.

- Expand your goals for sex from getting your rocks off to loving and servicing your partner—creating conditions for her to be able to feel safe enough to let go completely into paroxysms of pleasure. This is another area contributing to many men's feelings of inadequacy. In our porn-distorted world, men unfavorably compare themselves to impossible standards of beauty and performance, creating more pressure, insecurity, and discomfort in the bedroom. In Book 2, *Attracting and Nurturing Relationships That Work* (as well as in the Soulful Relationships retreats), we take a deeper dive into what makes a good lover.

## The Explorer/Discoverer

Discovering unexplored geographical places is another way in which men have excelled and served an important role historically. In our times there aren't that many frontiers left. Outer space (the "final frontier," a phrase popularized by the *Star Trek* TV show opening narration) remains unexplored, but the technology is not there yet, and the incredible physical, mental, and educational requirements would eliminate the majority of us from that role. For most of us, the inner space also remains unexplored. So you want to be a courageous explorer? Dare to go within. It will be so worth it and will change your life and all your relationships. And yes, it can even get you laid! Discover peace of mind, equanimity, quiet strength. Awaken and unleash your soulful power, without needing to prove it. Know yourself. You'll see how that increases your attractiveness and magnifies your sexual magnetism.

## The Builder/Creator

Instead of fuck or kill, make love and build.

Channel the impulse to build. Take on a project. There is so much that needs to be done. Get involved in building homes for the homeless, an urban garden, a meditation room at work, or a reforestation project.

Real power is ultimately spiritual. It comes from the depths of one's soul. It is the power of creation. Women are innately conduits for the forces of creation and are therefore naturally powerful. The power to engender life . . . what else could be more powerful?

For men, what is needed is a shift in thinking, a change in perception. Creation is not just about reproduction. Become a conduit for creativity, whether that's through art, construction, woodworking, gardening. That energy is available to us all. And like real power, it is a gift. The potential is inside of us. It takes opening to it, becoming channels for it and allowing enough time for its expression. But it won't happen much while watching TV!

The Problem-Solver is another expression of the Creator and a beautiful quality of the masculine. For those of you in relationship with women, however, be mindful of automatically switching on the problem-solving mode. Sometimes women just want to express and be heard.

> "WE ARE NOT PASSIVE COUCH POTATOES EITHER. IT IS NOT THE ESSENCE OF HUMANS TO BE PASSIVE. WE ARE PLAYERS. WE ARE ACTORS ON MANY STAGES.... WE ARE CURIOUS, WE ARE YEARNING TO WONDER, WE ARE LONGING TO BE AMAZED, TO BE EXCITED, TO BE ENTHUSIASTIC, TO BE EXPRESSIVE. IN SHORT TO BE ALIVE.... WE ARE ALSO NOT COGS IN A MACHINE. TO BE SO WOULD BE TO GIVE UP OUR PERSONAL FREEDOMS SO AS TO NOT UPSET THE MACHINE, WHATEVER THAT MACHINE IS. CREATIVITY KEEPS US CREATING THE LIFE WE WISH TO LIVE AND ADVANCING HUMANITY'S PURPOSE AS WELL."
> —MATTHEW FOX

## The Warrior

The warrior archetype is deeply embedded in our collective perceptions of what it means to be a man. Not only is it expressed through actual military warriors, but also through our first responders and sports figures.

As we create new and healthier ways to express manhood, we can also expand this energy to include the spiritual warrior who exhibits the courage to:

- Go within and slay his inner demons, his limitations.

- Be fiercely and unapologetically authentic in self-expression, no matter what.

- Dare to feel, and to express those feelings responsibly, with courage and compassion.

- Say no to injustice and abuse.

- Be willing to do the work of conscious relationship.

- Lead with integrity.

Direct the warrior energy to take on homelessness, poverty, pollution, injustice—all threats to our survival.

## The Destroyer

Men like blowing shit up. Conversations among men about sports can include startling warlike language and metaphors—perhaps serving as healthy channels for violent, destructive energies.

If you must destroy something, annihilate mediocrity, complacency, injustice, ignorance. Tackle your own ego. Obliterate your own fears, self-doubt, and self-imposed limitations. This will be much more satisfying—and beneficial—than a corporate takeover or military victory.

The prophet/activist/revolutionary has always stood for the death of systems that no longer work, at the same time advocating for the birth of something new. Think of Mandela, Gandhi, Havel, King, Jesus.

Take on a sacred destruction mission that will have both internal and external focus—your own hang-ups, whatever inhibits self-acceptance, and that which needs repair in the world. In Judaism, Tikkun Olam is a directive to help repair the world.

> "EVERY ACT OF CREATION IS FIRST AN ACT OF DESTRUCTION."
> —PABLO PICASSO

In Hinduism, destruction is a form of creation. Invoke Shiva, the sacred destroyer energy that must occur in order for new birth to happen. Shiva is also associated with the power of reproduction and regeneration, and one of his symbols is the lingam or phallus.

### The Nurturer

This has not been a traditional male role, but I include it here in order to name it and give permission. Is a gentle man less of a man? It takes a great deal of self-knowledge—and comfort in knowing you are a man—to be gentle and nurturing in a world that has labeled those qualities feminine.

What are some of the qualities we admire in men? Strength, courage, character, integrity, power, dependability, accountability, trustworthiness, honesty, humility, generosity. As we expand how we think of the masculine, can we add gentleness and nurturing?

In his book *Original Blessing*, Matthew Fox writes about the need to let go of the patriarchy "which creates one-sided citizens of women and men alike and culminates in violent living and violent relationships."[23] Our world is desperate for deeper, fuller, and more expansive expressions of what it means to be a man. As we let go of old, tired associations between the feminine and weakness, we can welcome again qualities such as nurturing into our expression. The truth is that we all have masculine and feminine energies coursing through us. And if you need examples of strength in the feminine, watch a YouTube video about men experiencing mechanically induced approximations of labor pains.

As the expression "mother bear love" alludes to, the feminine can be fierce. The Hindu goddess Kali is a powerful example. Like Shiva, she is a destroyer. In fact, she was called on by the male gods when they were losing a battle against demons. Whenever one was slain

> "I AM A MAN. A MAN SO MANLY THAT I FEEL A SHARP PAIN IN MY TEETH WHEN SOMEONE SNAPS A PLANT STALK, NO MATTER HOW SMALL. A GIANT. A GIANT SO GIGANTIC THAT I CAN EMBROIDER A ROSE ON THE FINGERNAIL OF A NEWBORN BABY."
> —FEDERICO GARCIA LORCA

and a drop of blood hit the ground, another one would burst forth. As Kali scooped the drops of blood with her tongue before they hit the ground—the reason she is generally portrayed with her tongue sticking out—the battle was reversed and won.

The world will benefit from more loving, affectionate, and physically demonstrative males, including the males themselves.

## MEN AND POWER

Power is about having the balls to question your beliefs, rather than accepting blindly and unquestioningly what has been passed down through the generations, mostly by men with a distorted and limited view of masculinity.

Increasingly, more and more men are stepping into authentic power themselves, and welcoming balanced relationships and power dynamics with female partners. More secure in their own sexuality, they are not threatened by others' expressions of theirs. (Misogyny and homophobia are two sides of the same coin. The cultures and religions that prohibit homosexuality are the very same ones that oppress women.)

As has been proposed in these pages, we all need to find appropriate expressions of power. We have established that this does not mean being a doormat. Coming to terms with soulful power takes into consideration defending and protecting yourself and your loved ones, your property, and your country. But not by abusing your power.

A series on "man killers" in the Art of Manliness website identifies power—worldly, egoic power, in this framework—as one of the culprits: "Power is necessary, without it nothing would get done. Police officers wouldn't be taken seriously if they didn't have the power to arrest, countries could be invaded if they didn't have a military (or nuclear weapons) to defend themselves, and business managers couldn't accomplish nearly as much if they didn't have the power to hire and fire their people.... Properly harnessed power can be used to better the lives of our loved ones, associates, and society as a whole. But men must be vigilant in avoiding power's potential to canker their soul, blind them to unethical decisions, and bring about their downfall."[24]

In the next part, as we make our way through the Zone of Power, we encounter thirteen empowering acts, behaviors, and choices that heroes throughout the ages have encountered. All these paths to soulful power are congruent with the hero's journey and can support us on our journey to freedom.

## POWER PRACTICES

- What qualities do you associate with the masculine?

- What qualities do you associate with the feminine?

- Choose one of the re-envisioned roles above. Commit to trying it on and giving it expression for the next month or longer. For example, if you gravitate to the Protector, you might volunteer at the local animal shelter.

# PART V

## Paths to Soulful Power

# CHAPTER 26
## PATH OF FORGIVENESS

You've followed along through all the pitfalls of the ego and our human foibles, including our ambivalence toward power and its unhealthy expressions. In this next phase of the journey we explore thirteen qualities—paths that lead to soulful power. Embodying these, taking them on as life practices, will expedite your process of empowerment and lead to personal freedom. They are not easy, but can become second nature over time. They are the stuff of heroes.

### FORGIVENESS: POWER TOOL TO FREEDOM

As we have seen, Anakin Skywalker's metamorphosis into Darth Vader began at the moment he gave in to rage and went on a murderous, vengeful rampage upon his mother's death at the hands of slave traders. Talk about a major ego reaction! Wouldn't you think that with all that Jedi training, he would have had the presence of mind to count to ten or take a deep breath? That was his moment of choice.

Forgiveness, however, is not easy in a situation such as that—or even in less drastic situations. In many cases, forgiveness is nothing less than heroic. Yet, forgiveness is not really about the other person or parties. It is about freeing ourselves from the shackles of victimhood. As long as we harbor feelings of having been wronged, or hold on to any level of self-righteousness or victimization, we remain trapped in that experience. Like it or not, forgiveness is the only way out, the only way to fully complete the experience, leave the past behind and move on. Though the other party will also be freed by forgiveness, it is ultimately about freeing ourselves. We become bigger for it, and in freeing ourselves we reclaim our own power.

> FORGIVENESS IS ABOUT FREEING OURSELVES FROM THE SHACKLES OF VICTIMHOOD.

Maia, my former teacher, had a beautiful way to think about forgiveness. When we turn the syllables around in "forgive," she observed, we get "give for." We give others (and ourselves, which is often more difficult) the room to be human, to make mistakes, to be less than perfect. When we forgive, we give the other person the benefit of the doubt, instead of judging them.

When we take things personally, when we hold on to the feeling of having been wronged in some way, we forfeit our power. We effectively give others too much influence over our state of being.

In the past, one of my pet peeves was when someone cut me off in the fast lane, only to slow down. "Why?" I would ask myself in frustration. "Why didn't you just stay over in 'your' lane? I don't even mind you pulling up in front of me, but don't slow down!"

Whether the person is completely clueless and oblivious to what they just did or is doing it on purpose to aggravate me doesn't matter. If I allow myself to get all worked up in anger and frustration, I'm the one paying the price. It is my bile that is being released into my stomach, my blood pressure that is rising, my nervous system that is becoming unnecessarily stressed. If the person did it on purpose, they are actually getting off on having upset me. Anyone who enjoys playing such simple and stupid power games must have a pretty lame life, feel powerless in general, and is therefore worthy of compassion! If they are spaced out and barely aware, they are also worthy of compassion. Who knows what may be going on in their lives? Maybe they just got fired or have a loved one in the hospital. Extending to them the benefit of the doubt frees me from an unnecessary emotional trip.

And besides, if I am truthful, haven't I done the same or similar? Maybe not that same situation, but haven't I ever spaced out while driving and impacted others on the road? Of course I have. Walking a bit in their shoes softens the self-righteous edge of judgment—"I would *never* do that!"—and frees both of us.

For ancient Hawaiians, forgiveness was an important part of the process of conflict resolution. According to the *Hawaiian Dictionary*, the concept of *ho'oponopono* derives from two words: *ho'o*, which is equivalent to the English "to"; and *pono*, which can mean "goodness, uprightness, morality, duty, proper, right, just and correct."[25] Together they create the meaning "to make right, to correct, to amend."

Traditionally, ho'oponono was used as a means to address conflict or discord within the family. The process involved prayer, discussion, confession, repentance, mutual restitution, and forgiveness and involved the extended family. In recent times, Morrnah Simeona, a gifted Hawaiian healer, expanded the concept of ho'oponopono to include problem resolution among groups outside the family structure. She also used this concept as a self-help tool for emphasizing personal responsibility.

Since her death in 1992, one of her students, Stanley Hew Len, with the help of *Zero Limits* co-author Joe Vitale, has been spreading his version of ho'oponopono. As administrator of a psychiatric unit for the criminally insane in Honolulu, Len's treatment method initially consisted of repeating the phrase "I'm sorry. Please forgive me. I love you. Thank you." Often performed even without direct client contact, the practice reportedly brought about such dramatic healing among the inmates that it not only reduced staff turnover and absenteeism, it also led to the eventual closing down of the unit. He now offers seminars supporting people to improve the quality of their lives and teaches "100 percent personal responsibility," meaning we take responsibility for everyone's actions, not just our own. Basically, it is saying: If it's in them, it's in me.

The way the practice was taught to me—possibly in error—was "I'm sorry. I forgive you. I love you. Thank you." With all due respect to Len's work, and though I understand his philosophy of assuming ultimate responsibility and asking forgiveness even for others' actions, I prefer the version I learned because it acknowledges both sides. Sometimes the other party needs the experience of being forgiven.

The person who taught it to me experienced its effectiveness in a personal way. While serving on the board of a national nonprofit, he was asked to head a committee to find a replacement for the organization's charismatic founder, who was nearing retirement. Over the course of two years, every time they were close to making a recommendation, one of the committee members would inevitably find something wrong with the candidate and thwart the process. Frustrated and at wit's end, my friend decided to try ho'oponopono. Every time he'd think of the sabotaging committee member, rather than get upset or angry or frustrated, he would hold him in his mind's eye while repeating: "I'm sorry. I forgive you. I love you. Thank you." At the next meeting two weeks later, the guy unexpectedly announced that he had decided to step down from the search committee, opening the way for the search process to actually unfold.

Forgiveness is an unavoidable step on the road to both freedom and soulful power.

## POWER PRACTICE

- Who will you forgive today? Choose one person and write them a letter. Explain how their behavior affected you and what effects it had on your life. Share the negative feelings you initially had and how now, thanks to what you may have learned, you have become stronger. Communicate that you forgive them. Is this a communication you wish to actually deliver if you are able to do so?

# CHAPTER 27
## PATH OF GRATITUDE

Gratitude is a renewable energy. It is a magnetic, attractive, and transmutative force that becomes self-perpetuating, engendering even more things for which to be grateful. In Spanish, the word for "thank you," *gracias*, also means grace. We can say that gratitude is a state of being, a state of grace. Living in gratitude—a gratitude attitude—transmutes challenges and situations we wish had turned out a different way. By now we know these are learning opportunities, the grain of sand that transforms into a pearl. When we learn to be grateful for all of it—the good and the challenging—our hearts are filled with grace.

Recent scientific studies indicate that simple gratitude practices result in the activation of the hypothalamus, which affects stress levels and other regions of the brain associated with the release of dopamine, a "feel-good" neurotransmitter that also helps initiate action.[26]

Gratitude gives us the power to change any situation, or at least our attitude toward and experience of it. At first it is a practice, until it becomes second nature, a state of being. You might, for example, take on a practice of writing down three things each day for which you are grateful. Some choose to keep a gratitude journal. Even making a one-time list can be a powerful process and bring about this state of being.

At one point in my life I was feeling stuck, imprisoned by a situation. There seemed to be no graceful way out. Sitting on top of a hill in San Francisco overlooking the city and Golden Gate Park, all the way out to the ocean, I found myself compiling a list of things I didn't like about my life. After a while I could not think of anything else about my current situation, but I was on a roll and decided to keep going back, capturing anything I had made wrong, disliked, or felt bad about in my entire life. After a couple of hours there was nothing else left inside of me. I felt cleansed, emptied, purified. Spontaneously, I began to create a list of things for which I was grateful. That simple practice got me out of a funk and helped shift the way I perceived certain experiences. By the end of the process, in a very natural way, I began to notice on my gratitude list some of the very same things that had been on my "hate list."

As part of our practice we make it a point to remember how much we have to be grateful for. We remember, for example, that in our world, 734 million people live on less than $1.90 a day—and that number is expected to significantly rise again in 2020 due to the COVID-19 crisis.[27] That means that close to 10 percent (a decrease from 30 percent in 1990) of the population on the planet is still barely surviving at the physical level! And even among those of us fortunate enough to live in the developed world with a roof over our heads and access to education (not to mention plentiful food, electricity and water), a large majority is still caught up in a rat race trying to make ends meet at the end of the month—barely surviving and not living fully. Considering the fact that one in five adults in the world is still illiterate, the fact that you are reading this book about personal empowerment and spiritual transformation is quite a privilege. Viewed in this larger context, depression is a luxury.

Gratitude gives us power over every situation. It is contagious. We are not talking about an airy-fairy, saccharine, Pollyanna gratitude but an attitude that is raw and genuine and brings about thankfulness for the gift of being alive, for the privilege of being in a body.

Living in this way is freeing and requires only one sacrifice: we must give up our attachment to suffering, struggle, drama, and the underlying addiction to victim consciousness. As we will explore more in depth later, the word sacrifice means "making sacred." By letting go of this stuff, we make our life sacred, full of grace.

## POWER PRACTICE

- For the next week, or month, commit to making a gratitude list. Name three things each day for which you are grateful.

# CHAPTER 28
## PATH OF SELF-DISCIPLINE

There are three aspects to self-discipline relevant to this discussion: mental, emotional, and spiritual.

**Mental** self-discipline refers to the efforts required to disidentify with the ego. The way of soulful power requires constant vigilance. The ego is such a deeply ingrained part of us and can be so clever and subtle in its expression that much practice and self-awareness are necessary when we are on the path to self-mastery. Simply put, we no longer allow our ego to run amok. We take charge of our thoughts, our emotions, and our lives. When the ego starts feeling victimized or self-righteous, we learn to say, "Thank you, but no thank you. I choose to see it this other way." With practice, the ego's voice becomes gradually softer, less intrusive, and hijacks us less frequently. Thankfully, when it does hijack us, it is for a much shorter duration.

We begin by learning to identify the voices of ego—self-doubt, constant questioning, the ruthless inner critic, self-righteousness, the victim. We bust ourselves, name the dynamic, acknowledge its egoic source and recontextualize the experience. Besides vigilance, this requires self-discipline. Seeing it is one thing; having the will to do something about it, another.

Yes, everyone can do it. To let ourselves off the hook by saying "I have no self-discipline," is to let the ego win right off the bat, without even trying. We are throwing in the towel at the beginning of Round 1. That's the first battle. Vigilance can be learned, and self-discipline can be developed, one step at a time. Practice is all it takes. As we become more self-aware, we learn to correct our thinking. The good news is that, as with anything else, it gets easier. In the words of the famed dancer Martha Graham: "We learn by practice. Whether it means to learn to dance by practicing dancing or to learn to live by practicing living, the principles are the same. One becomes in some area an athlete of God."

**Emotional** self-discipline means that at the same time we give ourselves permission to feel all of our human emotions, we also employ self-discipline as to the manner and timing of their expression. We simply don't blurt out what's going on with us or splatter someone against the wall because we are upset and "have the right to our emotions." Part of the maturing process is learning how to express our emotions gracefully without the need to suppress them. When we make a conscious choice with regard to how to communicate these emotions so they are received and heard without ego, we succeed, not only in being heard, but in honoring ourselves and the other. **Spiritual** self-discipline means undertaking certain practices, such as meditation, on a regular basis. These practices help when the rubber meets the road, and we are about to get hijacked by the ego. They will buy us those precious seconds of self-awareness that allow us to transcend reactivity, bring choice back into the equation and exercise true power.

## RECLAIMING OUR POWER FROM ADDICTIONS

Taking care of ourselves and our bodies is part of the process of empowerment. We cannot be out of control in one area of our lives—whether it's sex, drugs, or food—and feel powerful. All addictions are disempowering. We forsake our power for a pint of vodka or Häagen-Dazs, another line, a bump, a swig, an orgasm, a shopping rush, a "like" on Facebook, or attaining the next level in a video game. We all know these are but temporary solutions. We feel better in the moment when we get our fix, our high, our rush, but eventually plummet into disempowerment and regret.

Yet, there is always hope, a way out, no matter how deep a hole we have dug ourselves into. It begins by recognizing the problem. Recognizing we are powerless is the first of the 12 steps in the Anonymous programs. For many this is a constant struggle, a day-to-day battle to reclaim power over a substance or behavior by attending 12-step meetings, getting the help and support necessary to remain free. We can exert our personal power, the power over ourselves and over genetic predispositions. Fundamentally, it is about reclaiming our power of choice. And that takes self-discipline at heroic levels.

It all begins with a choice—to see clearly, to become whole, to get help. One step at a time, as they say in recovery groups, you can get back your body, your health, your self-respect, your mind, your power. Of course, making a choice or a declaration is not enough in the vast majority of cases, although sometimes that is all it takes. If we need more help, we then take the appropriate actions and obtain the necessary treatment and support structures. We end certain relationships, if need be, and create new ones.

In order for change to occur, we must address the underlying values that drive our behavior. We must choose and then learn to value our health, our relationships, our future, our legacy, our family, our friends more than the immediate high, escape, or numbness we have sought.

Though it is controversial to say in the addictions field, we need to be mindful not to replace one addiction with another, even a preferable one, if we are going for ultimate freedom. Some people I know no longer struggle with that. They have been effectively freed from their addictive tendencies and can indulge in the occasional glass of wine. For most others, the path of self-mastery requires permanent abstinence from a certain substance—be it alcohol, nicotine, or sugar.

As supportive and critical in the treatment process as regular meetings are, power does not come from them. Power comes from within. The meetings provide support, community, and important reminders. Power comes from a Higher Power, or whatever language works best for you. Otherwise we end up replacing one addiction with another.

## NAVIGATING THE FRENZY

The first skill to develop is learning to identify when "the frenzy" is coming on. What are the signs in your case? When do you start feeling the pull, the obsessive thinking? When does the desire start gently rapping on the window and then banging on the door?

The time for choice is *before* the rap turns into a bang. That's our window of opportunity. *Before* we act on the frenzy, before we click "Buy" or pick up the phone or the pipe or the cigarette or the mouse or the remote control or the pint or the spoon or the bottle or the pills. Instead, we take a few deep breaths. All we are doing is putting action off for a bit. Ideally, we sit comfortably and close our eyes. We can still make the choice at any moment; we are just delaying it in order to take advantage of the opportunity, trying to glean the most out of it, to learn from it as much as possible. We notice whatever goes on as we slow down our breathing. What are we feeling? What are we longing for? What's really going on? Is there another feeling we are trying to avoid, perhaps an activity, something we don't want to do? Someone we don't want to think about? Are we feeling lonely or sad, like something is missing? Or are we angry or upset about something?

When taming the tiger of addictive behavior, going in is the way out. As long as we keep ignoring our underlying emotions and experience, we are doomed to act out in ways to cover things up. Yes, it's a lot of work, hard work that requires commitment and self-discipline. We are wrestling with nothing less than the alligator of our biology and our conditioning. And it is a heroic path, for we are taming our inner demons and fighting for our lives.

If doing it for yourself is not enough motivation at this point, then do it for your loved ones; do it for all of us—your fellow travelers, your country, the world. If you are reading this book that likely means that you are on a path of self-discovery and self-healing and that means we need you. We need you now more than ever, fully in your power. At this most critical point in our history, we need all of us on the journey.

> "SELF-REVERENCE, SELF-KNOWLEDGE, SELF-CONTROL—THESE THREE ALONE LEAD LIFE TO SOVEREIGN POWER."
> —ALFRED, LORD TENNYSON

Support will show up from surprising and unexpected sources. Guaranteed. The Universe has a vested interest in each of us.

## POWER PRACTICE

- Identify one recent example of a situation in which you felt the voice of self-doubt, or the ruthless inner critic, creeping in. How were you from the onset? How long did it take for you to intervene? How were you able to reframe? From the current vantage point, how would you coach yourself to reframe the situation and address that voice?

# CHAPTER 29
## PATH OF VULNERABILITY

There is power in conscious vulnerability. Once we attain it, we are so confident in our power that there is nothing to defend—we are not worried about others' opinions or about being attacked. On the other hand, if we need to prove we are powerful, it is safe to assume we are compensating for feeling powerless in some way.

One Buddhist story tells about a monk who was falsely accused of impregnating a young woman who faced being ostracized by the villagers for giving birth out of wedlock. The monk endures quietly the anger and judgment of the villagers; he does not deny, defend, or explain and even accepts the responsibility of raising the child, in spite of his innocence. As it tends to do, the truth eventually comes out when the real father returns. Without hesitation the monk returns the son to his parents even though he has raised him as his own for years. The monk was exonerated, but the point is that he was free all along and did not need exoneration. Even when he knew he was right and despite the injustice and lies being told against him, he remained silent. That is freedom. That is power. No need to defend; no need to explain. His state of being and self-worth did not depend on what others thought or how they felt about him. To be clear, this example does not deny or preempt the work we have been exploring in these pages. Before attaining such high states of personal freedom, we first go through other stages during which we learn what works and doesn't work for us, how to create healthy boundaries, how to communicate our needs with courage, clarity, and compassion.

Defensiveness is an intrinsic trait of the ego and characteristic of the human condition. We feel attacked, questioned, misunderstood, victims of injustice. We feel compelled to prove our innocence, our rightness. This is the case especially when confrontation triggers deep issues of identity—how we perceive ourselves. The question is: Why is how others see us important? The more we shift our focus internally, the less external validation is needed.

Robert would get upset every time his boss Miriam would give him feedback that he felt was unfair. He never spoke up about it even though they were also friends; his resentment built until it started affecting their relationship. By the time he came to a retreat, the situation had deteriorated further following a bad performance review. He felt betrayed by his friend and was considering quitting. Throughout the weekend he realized that every time he got feedback from Miriam it reminded him of his mother who, with good intentions, had set very high standards for him. As a single mother, she wanted to make sure her son did well in life. The message young Robert internalized, however, was that no matter what he did, it was never good enough. That was the core wound and identity his boss was unintentionally triggering. With this insight, and having begun the work necessary for unconditional self-acceptance, he was able to speak with his friend and apologize for his unconscious passive-aggressive behavior. She, in turn, was happy to honor his request that, when giving feedback, she would also affirm the positive aspects of his performance.

Not taking things personally is key. Not everything is meant to be an attack or hurtful or an affront to our integrity. Most often people are simply acting out their own pain. There is no need to take it on. Let them have their experience. Be compassionate.

*COMPASSION* MEANS TO "FEEL WITH" AND IS AN IMPLICIT QUALITY IN HEROES.

That is how they are able to place themselves at risk for the sake of another. Heroes know that sometimes people are just working out their own insecurities, issues of trust, or overcoming perceived powerlessness in themselves. Heroes practice reining in our projections about others' motives and no longer ascribe meaning to their actions. Who knows why people do the things they do, what's going on in their lives, or what they are projecting onto us?

This does not justify anyone's behavior, nor does it mean that we get to write off or ignore all the feedback that comes our way because people are just "projecting their stuff onto us." Which they are. We simply learn to put on our "seal suit" or, as the Cuban saying goes, *nos damos un baño en kimbombo*, meaning "we take an okra bath." In other words, we let things slide off us and don't get snagged by them.

However, there are aspects of others' mirroring that could have elements of truth that can support our own growth process, particularly when we receive the same feedback from more than one source. In that case, we take it in for honest consideration without making ourselves wrong or plummeting into failure or shame. Instead, we look at it as objectively as possible with self-compassion and a constant commitment to growth and self-improvement. This takes self-knowledge and a lot of work on oneself, but who else will or can do that for us? It is about our personal freedom, ultimately.

Compromise is often a necessary part, maybe even an inevitable part of life. This does not translate into personal loss or diminishment. One of the best contributions from the classic negotiations book *Getting to Yes* is the concept of "expanding the pie," a strategy also taught at the Harvard Negotiations Program. Most negotiations are a one-dimensional zero-sum game in which the bigger your share is the smaller mine will be. The problem is this assumes a limited pie, so of course are we going to go for as much of it as possible. Instead, we need to focus on expanding the pie, exploring the concerned parties' interests and alternatives, finding ways to add value to what is on the table.

This approach takes more work, to be sure. It also entails doing the work of empathizing with the other, getting off our stance of being right, putting ourselves in their shoes. We take a deep breath and extend the benefit of the doubt. We genuinely seek to understand why they feel a certain way. We ask questions rather than making assumptions.

Leanne and Tammy had been in a five-year relationship by the time they came to a retreat as a last attempt to save their relationship. They left with a much broader perspective on relationships, renewed hope, and a willingness to try again. As it turns out, understanding the ego, projection, and "turning the mirror around" helped shift the way they fought. Months later I ran into Tammy, and she shared a story. In the middle of revisiting an old argument, she suddenly had a moment of clarity; she paused and took a breath. Rather than go down the old, boring road they had treaded for years, she decided to try a new approach and imagined they were having the argument for the first time. Instead of taking things personally and defending her position, she asked, "Leanne, would you help me understand why you feel that way?" A real conversation ensued and for the first time they got through to the other side with mutual compassion, deeper understanding, and the possibility of change.

Being always on the defensive and high alert is no way to live. It leads to high levels of stress, cardiac failure, and other health problems. We also pay a heavy price in the area of intimacy and the quality of our relationships. This "me against the world" approach to life leads to feelings of loneliness and alienation.

Developing an attitude of genuine curiosity helps, to use the language of communications expert Amy Fox from Mobius Executive Leadership, an organization specializing in corporate trainings in negotiations and communications. "I wonder why they might feel that way?" is a much more open-ended approach rather than making assumptions and building a case. Normally we—that is, our egos—figure it all out unilaterally, having appointed ourselves as prosecutor, judge, and jury.

Let's start giving each other the benefit of the doubt, rather than assuming the worst motives. Let us consciously evoke compassion in ourselves and try walking in their shoes for a bit.

Although it may seem counterintuitive, authentic and vulnerable communication has great power. Normally we think of someone vulnerable as weak, but it can actually be the exact opposite. Dropping the defenses and being consciously vulnerable entails a certain level of self-knowledge, security, self-awareness, and self-acceptance, which are all foundations for personal power. And making ourselves open and vulnerable, behaving in a way that extends and elicits respect, tends to generate the same in the other.

This, of course, does not mean being naive or prematurely revealing our hand in negotiations, for example. We must always be mindful to analyze what is motivating our behavior. It is easy to slip into approval seeking, sympathy seeking, or avoidance of conflict.

Being defenseless is also about freedom. We free ourselves from having to carry around a heavy shield and armor, constantly on the lookout for the next attack. When we walk around defended and protected, we are actually walking around in fear. This does not mean we unconsciously or naively place ourselves in dangerous situations, whether that means walking in a dark alley alone at night or hanging out with mean-spirited, sharp-tongued people. It means there is no need to live life wearing emotional body armor. The more self-healing work we do, we attract fewer people like that into our lives, and we have fewer buttons for others to push. We become less and less likely to get snagged and react. As a result, we are able to reclaim the high levels of effort and energy that walking around in a highly protected state require.

> "VULNERABILITY SOUNDS LIKE TRUTH AND FEELS LIKE COURAGE. TRUTH AND COURAGE AREN'T ALWAYS COMFORTABLE, BUT THEY'RE NEVER WEAKNESS."
> —BRENÉ BROWN

## POWER PRACTICE

- Let's consider a recent experience where you felt your defensive walls come up. What did the other party say that got you? How did you feel? When else have you felt that way or similarly? What patterns do you notice? When looking underneath your reactive response, as Robert did in the example above, can you identify a personal wound that may have gotten triggered? What core identity issue did you feel was being questioned or challenged? The more heroes are willing to this work of identifying and healing old wounds, the less they find themselves triggered by others.

# CHAPTER 30
## PATH OF BELIEF

Messages about the power of belief have been coming to us from a multitude of sources. This concept is becoming ingrained in the culture, as evidenced by popular songs such as "When You Believe" from the animated film *King of Egypt*. For the last 150 years what has come to be known as the New Thought movement has been teaching us that our thoughts and beliefs influence our reality. Talk to any life coach, motivational author, or success speaker and they will likely say that if we want to reach some goal in our lives, we first have to believe we can attain it.

In the highest echelons of sports, the practice of visualization is now taught by sports psychologists with much success. Visualization is like advanced belief-making. To go beyond belief, we involve the senses. We see the desired outcome in our minds; we taste and feel it as if it were already happening.

Matthew Levy, a former colleague in the corporate consulting and leadership development field, was part of a college rowing team that was consistently worst in their league. One year, as fortune would have it, they were able to hire the former coach for the U.S. Olympic team who lived in the area and happened to be in between jobs. On the first day of practice, they were all ready to get in the water when, much to their surprise, the training session began with a visualization exercise. That ritual continued as an integral part of the training throughout the season, by then end of which they had moved from last to first place in the league!

Often when we watch top-level athletes being interviewed at some point they will say: "I always knew I could do it." What we are talking about here is not arrogance and does not come from repeating an affirmation a few times and thinking that that will work. It is much more than that. The belief becomes ingrained in the fabric of our psyche and turns into *knowing*.

"THE ONLY LIMITS OF POWER ARE THE BOUNDS OF BELIEF."
—HAROLD WILSON

To generate this type of belief, the more we can involve the senses and the emotions, the more effective the process and the better the results. In other words, we train our minds to feel the wind as we are heading down the slope, to see the time clock with our record-breaking time at the end of the swim, to hear the roar of the crowd as we make it across the finish line, to feel the elation of victory as we take our victory lap. Needless to say, that does not preclude actually doing the work at the physical level: running, swimming, taking the time to sit down and write or compose or learn photography.

Nevertheless, the power of visualization is impressive. An experiment by Professor L.V. Clark of Wayne State University yielded compelling results. He compared two groups of high school basketball players over the course of two weeks. One group practiced free throws daily while the other simply visualized doing the same. Both groups improved their performance.[28]

A similar study by Guang Yue of the Cleveland Clinic Foundation compared a group that actively worked out in the gym with another group that simply visualized the same workout. Yue measured a 30 percent increase in muscle mass among gym-goers and 13.5 percent increase among those using the visualized workout. That represented almost half of the results just by using the power of the mind.[29]

To skeptics who still claim there is no scientific basis for beliefs affecting reality and attribute its success to the placebo effect, I say, as long as it works, who cares?

Interestingly, when we analyze the origins of the word "power," we find it comes from the Latin *posse*, meaning "to be able to." Not surprisingly, that connection between "power" and "being able to" is evidenced in modern romance languages. In French, for example, *pouvoir* and in Spanish, *poder* mean both "power" and "to be able to." *Si se puede* is the affirmative form of the verb *poder*. Yes, we can. Similarly, in Russian, *mosch* means both power or force and "I can."

The word *magic* also has an interesting etymology. It comes from the Proto-Indo-European *magh*, which meant "to be able, to have power." That same connection can be seen in the etymology of *dynamic*, from the Greek *dynamikos*, meaning "powerful," which in turn comes from *dynamis* "power," the root of which is *dynasthai* "to be able, to have power." Relevant as well is the fact that *potential* and *possibility* both share the same root: *potentia* ("power"), originating from *posse* ("to be able"). To be able to what? To act. To do.

We could therefore say that power, potential, and possibility all refer to the capacity to act. In each case there is an implicit choice to be made. To be able to does not mean that we will do it.

If power means to be able to, then it follows that powerlessness means not being able to. When we find ourselves in a deep state of depression, we feel powerless, inert, unable to do anything. In fact, we are sometimes practically incapable of movement, so lacking in energy (another word for power) that we can hardly get out of bed or off the couch.

> THE SHIFT FROM POWERLESSNESS TO POWER BEGINS WITH CHANGING THE BELIEF "I CAN'T" TO "I CAN."

Given what we have established about the power of belief and the etymology of power, perhaps the shift from powerlessness to power begins with changing the belief "I can't" to "I can."

We can begin to tell ourselves: "I can handle this and much more than this. This too shall pass. I can handle it in a way that is congruent with who I am. I can take a stand for myself, for my truth, without needing to put any one down or needing to prove anything. I am because I can."

## POWER PRACTICE

- What is an old "I can't" pattern in your case? What kind of situations did it keep you from enjoying? Is it still active? When was the last time it got you?

# CHAPTER 31
## PATH OF SELF-EXPRESSION

The journey of self-discovery is the most important journey we can take. It is an inner journey, and a heroic one. The dragons to be slain are our own fears and insecurities and outgrown belief systems, behavior patterns, and life situations. The challenges to be overcome stem from familial, social, and cultural conditioning.

The journey is an ongoing one and entails identifying our own inner blocks—misunderstandings we bought into when we were very young: that we were not good enough, pretty enough, intelligent enough or fill-in-the-blank enough. We simply no longer have time for that. Holding on to those beliefs may have protected us in some way; otherwise we would not have stuck with them. They may have kept us in relative safety and protected us from perceived harm, but they no longer serve. If playing small kept us from risking failure, it also prevented us from fulfilling our potential.

Enough! No more stuffing ourselves into smaller and obsolete containers. No more hiding our light under a bushel. It is high time to come out—from whichever closet—as the uniquely magnificent beings we are.

There is not another being in this universe—or any other universe, for that matter—who has the unique genetic qualities and particular set of experiences that make each one of us who we are. If we do not bring that unique human potential to fruition, who will? So, where do you stand? Will you bring that unique potential forth? Will you give it full expression, holding nothing back?

Self-expression is about unleashing the soulful power within. It is about being the very best we can be. It is about us and has nothing to do with anyone else's power. Others' power cannot diminish us.

But there is a fine line between self-expression and attention-seeking behavior—the "Look at me!" syndrome.

Whether we are expressing ourselves or showing off egoically depends on the come-from: Are we on stage—literally or figuratively—because we must, because there is something in us that must be expressed, some talent or gift or message that must be shared because that is our essence and our purpose? Or is it because we need the approval, validation, or adulation of others?

EXTERNAL VALIDATION IS LIKE A CRACK ADDICTION: WE CAN NEVER GET ENOUGH.

Only we can answer that for ourselves, although it is often easy to feel the difference when watching a performance. In the latter case we are compensating for feelings of inadequacy or not being good enough. It is a bottomless pit that can never be filled. A hero's sense of worth comes from within.

Authentic expression is not about trying to impress others. It is about being ourselves in our fullness. Ironically, someone who knows themselves deeply, who has faced down their inner dragons of insecurities and self-doubt, and who is not concerned about the impression they are going to make, earns the recognition they no longer need.

Such is the effect of authentic personal power and magnetism. There is power in being ourselves to the fullest. No one can give that to us; nor can they take it away. Or do it for us. It is ours. It lives inside us. It can be grown, cultivated, and developed. Anyone has access to it. No one is off the hook here. We all have access to that source of power. It is as easy—and as difficult—as going within.

What holds us back from full self-expression? Shyness. Fear of being judged. Fear of making a fool of ourselves. Fear of failure. Fear of rejection. We keep peeling the layers of the onion and going deeper until we get to our core beliefs: ways of thinking about ourselves that developed when we were very young— sometimes even at a preverbal stage—and which have no basis in current reality. Core beliefs were the result of a misunderstanding by a young and uninformed mind: "There is something wrong with me." "I am stupid," or what has been termed the "Reverse L'Oréal:" "Why? Because I'm not worth it." Being able to identify these core beliefs and fears is more than half the battle, as well as realizing that they are normal and a part of the human experience. We all have some version of them. One of the gifts of breathwork, incidentally, is that it helps dissolve them at the source.

Are you tired of playing small, feeling insignificant?

Will you be the best you can be, or not?

It is that simple.

Of course, the question then becomes, who are you?

The hero's journey is about self-discovery and self-expression.

Embark on it.

Embrace it.

Dive into it.

Trust.

Your heroic quest will be supported.

---

"BELIEVE IN YOURSELF.
YOU GAIN STRENGTH,
COURAGE, AND
CONFIDENCE BY EVERY
EXPERIENCE IN WHICH
YOU STOP TO LOOK
FEAR IN THE FACE....
YOU MUST DO THAT
WHICH YOU THINK YOU
CANNOT DO."
—ELEANOR ROOSEVELT

---

## POWER PRACTICE

- Think of a recent time when you felt the need for external validation. What was going on beneath the surface leading to it? Were you feeling uncertain or insecure? When have you felt that before? Was there a previous similar situation? Do you see a pattern forming?

# CHAPTER 32
## PATH OF GENEROSITY

So much of our culture is geared toward supporting selfishness: getting our own, taking what's ours and sometimes what isn't—such as land and natural resources—even if it means we need to invade someone else's country to do so. The brilliant inventor Nikola Tesla had plans to develop free energy for all. However, his funding was withheld by his investor, J.P. Morgan, because Morgan sought profit. Greed and the profit motive won that round, as did Tesla's competitor and nemesis, Edison.

As the word egotism indicates, selfishness is of the ego. Earlier we saw that the "inner brat" is the voice that says, "I want what is mine and I want it now!"

All this talk of self-expression might feel to some like a form of selfishness. Again, it depends on where we are coming from. The highest way we serve others and the world is by being the most that we can be, by evolving to the highest levels of consciousness possible. That will have a positive ripple effect and impact others.

One of the books I often recommend at retreats is *The Universe is a Green Dragon*, by Brian Swimme, a physicist and cosmologist who in a very readable way has applied the rules that govern the cosmos to the human experience. One of those principles is Cosmic Generosity. When a supernova explodes and gives up its form, as a result of that ultimate act of generosity, stars, planets, suns, and moons are born. Life occurs. Reminding us that we are made of the very same elements present in the stars—in a literal, not poetic, sense—Swimme concludes that as star beings, Cosmic Generosity is inherent to our natures. We too have that desire to give ourselves away.

Selfishness brings about contraction and limitation and stems from the belief, the underlying fear, that there is not enough. In contrast, generosity expands who we are and our sphere of influence. There is enough, more than enough, so I can freely share myself and our stuff with others. It is a much more empowered place in which to live. The path to power through generosity inspires us to release the supernova that is inside of us. Heroes do just that: give themselves away.

Similar to self-expression, we learn to express generosity authentically, not as a compensation for any perceived lack, or as in the case of generosity, around issues of self-worth. So many people who attend retreats initially come with a subconscious pattern of conditional giving. They have learned patterns of giving with an expectation of receiving something in return: acceptance, recognition, or pseudo-love. In relationships we often see this pattern in the "Rescue Syndrome." Some people derive self-worth by "fixing" others. Needless to say, feeling compassion for and helping others is an honorable thing. When it is driven by a lack of self-esteem or some other unconscious dynamic, it becomes a problem and limits the possibility for deep intimacy and fulfillment in relationships.

Heroes give because the desire to do so bursts out of us and gives us joy, not out of need to gain acceptance or validation. That strategy is ineffective and also doomed to fail.

"MAN'S POWER LIES IN GIVING. HE MUST LEARN TO GIVE AS NATURE GIVES. EACH HALF OF A CYCLE ETERNALLY GIVES TO THE OTHER HALF FOR RE-GIVING. NATURE FOREVER UNFOLDS INTO MANY FOR THE PURPOSE OF REFOLDING INTO ONE. EACH INDIVIDUAL MUST MANIFEST THIS UNIVERSAL LAW."
—WALTER RUSSELL

## POWER PRACTICE

- Practice generosity. Give someone an anonymous gift, without expectation of acknowledgment or reciprocation. This could be leaving a wrapped book or a greeting card with an inspirational message on a co-worker's desk. Or coming up with a simple message of reassurance or encouragement and a simple gift (an amulet or stone, for example) and leaving it on a park bench or subway seat.

# CHAPTER 33
## PATH OF COMMITMENT

One of the quotes that participants of Soulful Purpose retreats find most helpful is from William Hutchinson Murray's *The Scottish Himalayan Expedition*: "Until one is committed, there is hesitancy, the chance to draw back, always ineffectiveness. Concerning all acts of initiative (and creation), there is one elementary truth the ignorance of which kills countless ideas and splendid plans: that the moment one definitely commits oneself, then providence moves too. A whole stream of events issues from the decision, raising in one's favor all manner of unforeseen incidents, meetings, and material assistance, which no man could have dreamt would have come his way. I learned a deep respect for one of Goethe's couplets: 'Whatever you can do or dream you can, begin it. / Boldness has genius, power and magic in it!'"

From the Latin *mittere* we get both *promise* (*promittere*, "to send forth") and *commitment* (*committere*, "to send together"). We can thus say that when we make a *promise* we are sending forth our intention. When we *commit*, we send forth an intention together with a decision; we take a step further and send a clear message to the Universe of our decision to take some action.

Once we make a commitment, then the Universe completes the circle and responds. I have seen this happen so many times around retreat participation. Often money will show up in miraculous ways, at just the right time, from unexpected sources, once person has committed to a goal and made a clear choice.

My favorite story involves Kara, a single mother who at the time was in her twenties; her son must have been a year old. After I announced an upcoming two-week long residential retreat in Santa Fe, she came up to me and explained: "I have no idea how I could possibly afford something like this; I'm on food stamps right now. But I know I need to be there and I'm coming." In all honesty, knowing her situation I did not give a lot of weight or consideration to her declaration. What a humbling life lesson it turned out to be, one which has also impacted countless people with whom I have shared the story!

As it turned out, a few weeks later, while already in New Mexico getting ready for the retreat, I received a frantic voicemail: "Christian, I hope you saved me a space. You won't believe what just happened." Long story short, years earlier an old boyfriend had developed a drug problem and taken some of their money to support his habit. After breaking up with him, she had lost contact and never thought she would hear from him again. Well, he'd gotten clean, was in the process of making amends, tracked her down and sent her a check, which turned out to be precisely the amount of money she needed for the retreat and to get herself there! In the face of her willingness and trust—not to mention the miracle, for lack of another word—an exception was made and even the child came to the retreat.

More recently, Esther, a more mature colleague with an established relationship with trust, was debating whether or not to come to my annual retreat in Hawaii. She said yes to herself and asked for a sign: at the 11th hour, $11,000 she was not expecting from a previous consulting client showed up, months later, in her bank account.

These are good examples of why we all need to take a deeper look at trust.

## POWER PRACTICE

- What is one thing you have been delaying or procrastinating on—a project, perhaps a class to develop a new skill or hobby? Will you commit to giving it expression? First make the commitment and then set a timeframe with a deadline. By when will you do it? Whom will you share this with to keep yourself accountable? Start simply. Break it down into smaller chunks. So rather than committing to clean your office, commit first to cleaning out the top drawer in your desk. Make it doable and repeat the process. Or if you've longed to write a book, commit to the process, and start with a simple outline. The power of that will awaken your creativity, and you're off and running.

# CHAPTER 34
## PATH OF TRUST

Many teachings tell us that love is the opposite of fear, and those connections are clear. We approach life, people, and circumstances from either of those two places. As we have seen, courage—what many would identify as the opposite of fear—comes from the French word for "heart." In some ways, though, to me it feels that the opposite of fear is trust. At times when I have been nearly incapacitated by fear I was not remotely able to summon the feeling of love. Instead, it was the salve of trust that got me through it.

Trust is not cross-your-fingers-close-your-eyes-and-hope-it-works-out blind faith. It is closer to a sense of knowing. Trust leads to power because it is key in helping us move through fear.

## MOVING THROUGH FEAR

Fear, in one of its many facets, is what has kept us stuck in stifling jobs, soul-devouring mediocrity, suffocating relationships—in "lives of quiet desperation," as Thoreau wrote. The issue of fear and how to transcend it almost always comes up at Soulful Purpose retreats.

Contrary to what many believe, fearlessness does not mean the absence of fear. It means we no longer give fear the power to hold us back. How do we do that?

I have always had a sense of mission, and knew that I had to overcome my incapacitating fear of public speaking if there was any chance I could fulfill that mission. Reclaiming my power in this area became an imperative.

The first thing that needed to happen was a shift in my own values. In order for me to override my fear and speak in front of a group, the vital importance I attributed to my sense of mission had to become a more powerful driver than the disabling fear I felt, in order for me to override it and be able to stand in front of a group. It's easy to surmise that underneath any fear of failing or ridicule I might experience when speaking in public was my need for acceptance. Therefore, the need to express my mission had to be valued more than the need for acceptance.

Second, I made a choice and, based on that choice, took action. I signed up for a course in public speaking. For fourteen weeks on Thursday night I would have to get up and deliver three two-minute talks. How I detested that! Come Monday night I was already not sleeping well in anticipation of the dreaded Thursday. Yet the more I did it the less of a big deal it became.

Years later I was exposed to Susan Jeffers's book *Feel the Fear and Do It Anyway*. Her model is a series of concentric circles, the central one representing our original zone of comfort—the level at which we are presently comfortable communicating with others and being in the world. Every time we take a step—no matter how small—out of that zone of comfort, we stretch those boundaries and become established at the next zone of comfort.

It is that simple. If we are willing to place ourselves in slight discomfort, undertaking small actions—even baby steps—each week, picking up the phone and making a call or whatever the case may be, at the end of the year we are established way beyond our original comfort zone. And the good news is we never go back to that original comfort zone.

Saying no to fear is a heroic act. No longer are we willing to be held back by anything. This willingness to delve deep and face our own inner demons results in dramatic growth.

By implementing these simple techniques, I transformed my incapacitating fear into self-empowerment. These days I frequently speak to large groups. And I am actually a professional speaker who gets paid well for doing so! I still have to deal with the occasional butterflies in the stomach prior to getting on stage, but once I am off and running, everything is OK. I am even able to enjoy myself! More importantly, I know that through my words real human lives are being impacted. I am living my mission.

## LEAP!

"Leap and the net will appear," wrote Julia Cameron in *The Artist's Way.*

Or better yet, wings will sprout, and we will soar!

Why should you trust? Life, the Universe, have a vested interest in your blossoming, in being the most you can be, particularly at this point in our collective evolution. We need you fully in your power now!

I want to share a story that I have only told in select settings, mostly my Soulful Purpose retreats. I deeply value my privacy. I now choose to override such tendencies because of the possibility that it will prove helpful for others.

The evolving (or is it devolving?) global economic situation has forced many people to take a closer look at their lives and livelihoods. COVID-19 suddenly, dramatically, and rudely eliminated millions of jobs. But many of these jobs, when looked at honestly and openly, provided only an illusion of security and fell somewhere on the spectrum between comfortable but unfulfilling and soul-devouring. With the wake-up effect that comes from facing their mortality, many are feeling the call to step more fully into their life purpose and are exploring roles of teachers and healers. Yet they worry about how the bills will get paid if they do so. As scary as these situations may seem, at a soul level, they can be a gift, a deep blessing.

When I first met my former spiritual teacher, I was doing just fine for myself, thank you very much! In fact, my life was enviable. I had a cushy job making good money, a condo on the water in Miami Beach (right as the South Beach renaissance was taking off), a sporty car, a handsome lover, original art on my walls, Armani suits. I had good friends and was sought after socially and professionally. In spite of all this I was not happy. As the dreaded "three-oh" approached, I began to question what it all meant.

I was working in the community relations department of a psychiatric and addictions hospital, at a time when the insurance companies were beginning to tighten the screws. I started to see practices that left a bad taste in my mouth, such as people admitted into inpatient treatment when they might have had more success in outpatient treatment. Others were kept longer than necessary as long as their benefits permitted. Increasingly, the industry was becoming more bottom line-oriented, and in direct proportion, I was getting disillusioned with my work.

One day as I sat by the waterfront pool in my condo, a neighbor came down, saw that I was reading something spiritual, and struck up a conversation about breathwork and a teacher with whom he was studying. He invited me to attend an upcoming weekend intensive, "A Call to Greatness." My response was immediate: When and how much? I was ready and knew somewhere inside myself that this is what I had been waiting for.

A few months later, my life was opened up and turned inside out and upside down by Maia, her teachings, and my first breathwork experience. I knew I wanted more and immediately signed up to do ten private sessions with her—the last person to do so, as she was moving on from that work. At the same time, I took whatever advanced classes she was offering. I began to learn about meditation, teachings from the East, the perennial philosophy, the evolution of consciousness, and deeply insightful and practical information about what makes us tick as human beings—stuff which, ironically, I never got as a psychology major in college or in my previous religious upbringing.

Things unfolded rapidly. A couple of months later at a New Year's retreat on Marco Island on the west coast of Florida, she experienced a transformative moment that she translated as a leap in consciousness and a call to assume the role of guru in a traditional Eastern model.

Yikes. For many of her students the changes proved too much and most of them scattered. This was not surprising, since most of us had never even heard the word *guru*, or had no idea what it meant in a spiritual context or what that relationship entailed.

Six months later I was sitting on a plane, along with Maia and five other disciples, looking out the window as we crossed the continent and then the Pacific en route to Hawaii, where she had been led to move. Having sold my car and condo (prematurely from a worldly perspective) and given away most of my belongings (except for my books and my Armani suits, which tells you a bit about my attachments). I was able to bring into this budding spiritual community several thousand dollars.

My credit cards, which had just been completely paid off in preparation for my leap into the unknown, were used to purchase all of our plane tickets. The plan was that they would be paid off as soon as the retreat and seminar work took off. Well, guess what? The work never took off. By the end of the summer, Maia had asked one person to leave, two others had left of their own accord, and the last two were asked to step back temporarily. For the next year, she and I traveled alone and lived off my credit cards as we moved back to the mainland and tried unsuccessfully to launch the work first in southern California.

The creditors, predictably, soon began to call, as we could no longer effectively juggle the payments. One by one my cards got canceled. We got evicted from the furnished corporate apartment we were renting, and somehow were able to get into an unfurnished one in Redondo Beach, where we slept on our inch-thick exercise mats for a couple of months until we had to leave that one as well, tails between our legs. When things got critical, we escaped north to the Bay Area, where I ended up living for the next twenty years. At one point we slept in the car for a week, taking four-dollar showers at a neighborhood YMCA in the mornings. We were homeless.

I cannot begin to convey how challenging that time was for me. First my identity was being disassembled as, one by one, all symbols of worldly success were stripped away. That was hard enough, but worse was carrying the responsibility for a person who was still in the midst of some kind of spiritual transition that intermittently rendered her dysfunctional in the world. At the same time, I was the sole focus of her piercing, take-no-prisoners, ego-slaying mind. I still don't know how I managed to make it through that year.

Yet the experience proved invaluable, in more than one way. The one that is relevant here has to do with trust. Over the months I pawned the rest of my stuff—including a stereo system, all my CDs, even a chain my best girlfriend had given me in college—so that we would have money to eat or a place to sleep for the night. Yet no matter how bad things got, we never missed a meal. Not once. Each time we were down to just a few dollars something would happen, and money would show up, often from an unexpected source—a refund, a gift. As a result, I learned to trust. I now know in the core of my being, at a cellular level, that I'm going to be fine and will be taken care of. That alone was worth the harrowing experience.

The whole point of telling you the story is to assist and inspire those of you facing the quandary, the niggling question of "how will I take care of myself if I follow my soul's calling?" My goal is to reassure you that when we answer the call to our highest, whatever that may be, we will be supported. I also hope that it will help make your journey toward trust easier than mine.

"WHEN I DARE TO BE POWERFUL, TO USE MY STRENGTH IN THE SERVICE OF MY VISION, THEN IT BECOMES LESS AND LESS IMPORTANT WHETHER I AM AFRAID."
—AUDRE LORDE

Different spiritual teachers and seers explain that what is going on now in terms of the evolution of consciousness in our planet not only has an effect on the quality of life here on Earth but has overriding implications in terms of consciousness coming into form. Viewed from that perspective, how can the Universe not offer support when a soul makes a choice that will affect not only its own evolutionary process but the many lives that will be touched through its efforts?

Trust that you will be taken care of in your journey of empowerment, if and when your quest for authenticity requires that you leave a personal or professional situation. Needless to say, act smartly and mindfully, especially if there are others who depend on your income. You may want to have something else lined up before quitting your job. Or not. You may be at a place where your soul is being squelched. Be mindful here about egoic tendencies to feel victimized, as well as the desire to escape. There may be an opportunity to grow and practice empowerment by staying in the cauldron of a challenging situation. Furthermore, when we stand in our soulful power as our authentic selves, the world tends to align, and situations tend to change.

A process of discernment is recommended before taking action, one which can involve a trusted confidant or council of advisors. Ultimately, however, no one can tell you what to do. Others can help you get clear, but the choice is yours to make—and yours alone.

What I know is that the world does align once we get to that point of no return, when we have had it and are no longer willing to forfeit our power or sell out on ourselves for some illusion of security or out of fear of conflict or that we will not find someone else to love us. Trust!

In the film *Indiana Jones and the Last Crusade*, the hero is faced with three deadly challenges he must master before reaching his goal, the Holy Grail. In the final test, he must figure out a way to get across a deep chasm, on the other side of which the grail sits. It's only once he takes a "leap of faith" and steps into the void that the hidden stone shows up and meets his foot. In Rumi's words, "As you start to walk on the way, the way appears."

One final thing to highlight about trust. One of the reasons we have a hard time trusting each other is that we look at trust through different facets of a prism. Keith Ayers of the Integro

Leadership Institute in Australia suggests there are four elements of trust:[30]

1.  Reliability is the most basic element and refers to being accountable, keeping our word, doing what we'll say we'll do.

2.  Openness involves receptivity, the ability to listen and allow room for disagreement.

3.  Acceptance refers to a nonjudgmental attitude.

4.  Congruence refers to consistency and alignment between thoughts and action. It means "walking our talk." It is probably the least known aspect, and yet in some ways the most important. As such it warrants further discussion.

## POWER PRACTICES

- Rate yourself on a scale from 1 to 10 on reliability, openness, acceptance, and congruence (1 = completely untrustworthy and 10 = trustworthy all of the time.)

- Which of the four types of trust is your strongest suit? Which requires some work and development?

# CHAPTER 35
## PATH OF CONGRUENCE

Congruence refers to the alignment of the internal with the external. Our thoughts, beliefs, and feelings match and are consistent with our behavior and actions—what we say and do. It also includes authentic self-expression: We are who we are no matter what the setting or who we are with, as opposed to being one way at home and acting differently at work, for instance.

Whenever we are other than our genuine selves or keep ourselves small to maintain the peace or out of fear of conflict, we allow our power to leak. Soulful power can only be experienced when we come from a place of authenticity.

The word authenticity originates from the Greek *autos* meaning "self" and *hentes,* meaning "doer, being," thus simply, "being ourselves." Not being ourselves requires a lot of work. What a relief just to be who we are at all times, in every setting, aligned in what we say, believe, think, do, and act! No need for façades. No need for pretense. What freedom in not having to split off or

> "PERSONAL POWER IS STRAIGHTFORWARDNESS THAT WORKS. IT ACHIEVES WHAT NO AMOUNT OF STRATEGIC POWER CAN. TRUE COMMUNICATION OF THOUGHTS AND FEELINGS. PERSONAL POWER DEPENDS FIRST ON SELF-KNOWLEDGE; WITHOUT THAT IT IS AN EMPTY EXERCISE."
> —ROBERT KAREN

compartmentalize aspects of ourselves! To be who we are. All the effort and energy we spend trying to put on a face, pretending to be something we are not, having to remember what we said to this one or that one is suddenly freed up. That unleashed power can be applied to other areas of our lives, toward our growth, success, and self-discovery.

As Robert Karen's quote illustrates, in order to be congruent, to be ourselves in the world, we must first know who we are. The process of going within, cultivating our garden, doing the work on issues of self-worth is unavoidable if we are going to step into power in a healthy way.

How do we know if we are being ourselves? If we drop in and are honest with ourselves, we just know. A good question to ask is "How do I feel afterward?" Interestingly, no one can tell us who we are, but anyone with a little insightfulness and sensitivity can usually tell when we are not being ourselves. It's as if we had built-in authenticity (and bullshit) radars. We can feel when something is off or does not feel quite right.

Needless to say, being congruent does not mean we set aside respect and throw all sense of decorum out the window. It is not about an arrogant, rebellious, or adolescent acting out: "Screw you, world! This is who I am; deal with it!" Compassion and consideration are always present in our minds, as is practicing the Ethic of Reciprocity, or Golden Rule. Found in some form in every religion, it teaches us to treat others as we would like to be treated.[31]

Striking a balance between congruence and compassion entails a radical commitment to self-awareness, always being on the lookout for egoic needs to one-up someone, to establish the upper hand in a relationship or put someone in their place. Power dynamics can be very subtle and most often take place beneath the surface of conscious awareness. But they are there.

Besides freeing up energy, being congruent leads us on a path to power by reinforcing our self-worth. Each time we are genuinely ourselves and speak our truth in the world bolsters our sense of self, which makes us even more empowered and therefore more apt to be congruent. It is a self-affirming and self-perpetuating process. We stand free, not needing anyone's approval or validation, even in the face of judgment or opposition. Not out to prove anything to anybody, we simply stand in our power.

Being incongruent creates a state of inner conflict. Often, in order to try to reduce that discomfort, we numb out in one of the many ways we have mastered numbing out. Another strategy involves using tools in the ego's repertoire: denial, rationalization, blaming, justification. Being inauthentic completely saps our power. At some level we know and are disgusted by it.

Part of the reason for my painful adolescence was that I was living a lie. My secretive double life took its toll, resulting in depression and feelings of alienation. These days I am completely myself. I speak and write about being gay. However, this does not mean I feel obligated to wear a rainbow sticker on my forehead everywhere I go. My sexual orientation is but one part of who I am. I can be selective about when and where to bring it up. (Incidentally, for those not having to deal with coming out, it is relevant to note that it is not an isolated experience but a constant, ongoing process.) In corporate settings, for example, I choose not to introduce what could be a potential distraction, interfering with my effectiveness in the short time I usually have with a client. I do not feel as though I am hiding, lying, suppressing myself, or relinquishing my power in any way. On the other hand, if I were doing diversity training, my being gay would be pertinent and that would be a different story. As always, we have choice.

*A Call to Greatness*, one of Maia's books, evolved out of an eight-week class titled "A Course in Congruence." Much of her work was initially about that topic. The book opens with one of my favorite stories from her life; I can't think of a better to illustrate and inspire congruence:

> There were 50 participants in the training, plus one trainer and
> two apprentice trainers. I realized that I was not the only one
> who did not want to be there soon after my arrival. The buzz
> in the ladies' room, in the lobby area, and in the training room

itself, as we waited for the seminar to begin, was all about that. Since we were all there to earn needed college credits, nearly everyone was complaining about having to be there.

At the first break—as we stood outside in the soft Florida evening—the trainees continued to complain about being there; and they began to voice their judgments of the trainer, the material, the room, the distances they had come, the bad coffee, etc. We all obviously thought we were there only to fulfill the contractual requirements for State Board Certification. Without knowing it, I was there for a much more important reason.

The sessions were held on Friday evenings, and all day on Saturdays and Sundays. After the trainer opened the first session by outlining all of the value we would be receiving during the next days, we sat in a large circle and, one-by-one introduced ourselves to the group. At some point in that long process, I heard a silent voice say to me, "Teach a Course in Congruence." And I felt myself immediately respond with a silent, inner YES! I had never heard the word "congruence" before, but I was highly energized by the direct guidance, and I knew, without a doubt, that it was another pivot in my process.

Rather than stay overnight in Pompano, I drove back and forth to Miami between sessions. When I arrived home late that Friday night, I spent two hours referencing my psychology texts, trying to find the word "congruence." I finally found it in the works of Carl Rogers. It meant "an accurate matching of the inner experience with the outer expression." It meant "authenticity," "genuineness," "realness." I was thrilled. That is exactly what my own process had brought me to, and I was to teach it to others.

At some point during the Saturday morning session of the training, I decided that I was going to be congruent through-out the seminar, as an experiment. The process that ensued as a result of that decision was fascinating, uncomfortable, and truly enlightening.

The teaching was uninspired. The group energy was very low. And there was obviously an unspoken agreement among the participants that everyone would just endure the experience, go through the motions in the training room and vent their frustrations during breaks and mealtimes. It was obvious that there was a generalized agreement that it was all a waste of time and a meaningless endeavor. As the lunch hour approached, nothing of substance or real value had been offered in the seminar, and the trainer had, a few times, reiterated the list of specific communications skills we could expect to gain there. I raised my hand, was called on, stood up and stated my name (which was the prescribed protocol), and in a well-modulated voice, said, "I really do not want to be here, but since I am here, I sincerely want to receive value from the seminar. Six hours have already passed, and I have received none. When will we begin to get some of that information from the list that you have read a few times?"

The trainer's face became a study in surprised, speech-less confusion. He did not know how to react; he could think of nothing to say. I HAD BROKEN THE SILENT AGREEMENT. A hush had fallen over the room. The other participants seemed breathless, shocked, ill-at-ease. The trainer laughed nervously, assured me that we would begin in earnest after lunch and dismissed the group. I WAS SHUNNED. As we left the room, everyone averted their eyes and nervously distanced themselves from me, as they invited each other to lunch. Interesting, I thought. I contemplated the implications of my demonstration as I ate my lunch alone.

Returning after lunch to the Holiday Inn where the training was being held, I entered the ladies' room. The conversations all stopped, and a silence was maintained until I left. Interesting, I thought. And that is the way we continued throughout the first weekend. From time to time during the seminar, I would feel a real need for self-expression about what was happening or was not happening in the seminar, and I would communicate that with courage, self-discipline, and gracefulness. On each occasion, my congruence elicited a reaction similar to the one that followed my initial demonstration.

The trainer became a bit paranoid. I could tell he was anticipating my comments or questions with an obvious level of dread. I was so unpopular that I had a difficult time finding a partner on the many occasions we needed one to do a process. I ate lunch and dinner alone and stood by myself at break. When they were outside the training room, I could hear the other participants still complaining about the training, the room, the distances they had come, the coffee, etc. But once they reentered the room, they put on a "good" act—acting as though they were very interested and fully aligned with the trainer and everything that was going on there. I had seen this happening all of my life, and it had always been abhorrent to me. But this time, I did not have to pretend in any way that I was a part of it. Neither did I have to feel rebellious and reactive about it. I merely maintained my own sense of self and allowed myself to be authentic and natural—just me, with none of that other nonsense added. And although the experiment was uncomfortable for me, I felt a wonderful freedom.

During the week back in Miami—between the two weekends in Pompano—I reflected on the experience a lot. I realized that I had been living congruently to a great degree since my moment of truth in 1984. And even though I was fully committed to complete the experiment I had begun, my discomfort level was high; I dreaded returning for the second weekend of the seminar. On Friday, during the long drive to Pompano, I wondered if there had been a change of heart on any of their parts regarding me that week. When I entered the ladies' room before the first session, silence fell over the room again. Nothing had changed. We continued the seminar. I continued my experiment.

Sometime during that second Saturday afternoon session, an interesting thing happened. The young man who sat across from me in a process we were doing said, "I want to tell you that I really admire you for what you have been doing here. I wish I could do that." After that, some others who partnered with me also made unsolicited statements, which included the words "admire," "respect," "honor," etc. Interesting, I thought. (But I was still left alone during breaks and lunch and dinner hours.)

At some point on Sunday, I began to be chosen for processes, rather than having to wait until everyone else had been chosen and being the one who was "left over." At one point, one of the apprentice trainers asked me if she could be my partner. Instead of doing the process, she spent the whole time telling me how much she admired what I was doing and asking me questions about it. Very interesting, I thought.

After all the teachings had been done, all the processes completed and the final test administered, we began the closing session, which was the graduation ceremony. Once again, we sat in the large circle, as we had on that first Friday evening. The trainer stood at a podium just inside the circle at one end of the room. He would call the name of a participant, the participant would rise, walk to the podium, and receive his/her certificate of completion from the trainer, who would shake the participant's hand. Everyone else would applaud.

Since my name (at the time) was Riley, most of the names had already been called before I heard mine. With apprehension I rose from my chair and began to walk the length of the large room toward the trainer. My mind raced. My body was tense. The ordeal of the past week had obviously taken its toll. THEN A TOTALLY UNEXPECTED SERIES OF EVENTS BEGAN TO HAPPEN ALL AT ONCE. The trainer stepped out from behind the podium and began to walk toward me, his hand outstretched; applause broke out all around the room, with such feeling, volume, and intensity that it startled me. Then EVERYONE STOOD UP. I was receiving a standing ovation!

As the grinning trainer met me in the middle of the room and shook my hand with surprising vigor, some of the participants whistled, some let out catcalls, some laughed and some cried. I was astonished. I was speechless. I began to laugh and cry with them.

They left their chairs and converged in the center of the room and gleefully began to retrace the course of my earlier communications and their responses to them. It was great fun for the whole group—even for the trainer. I was not gleeful. Instead, I was flooded with feelings of humble amazement. I had become their hero, out of the very truth of myself.[32]

The story illustrates the power of one and how authenticity inspires and makes a difference. How many times have we been on the proverbial sidelines, judging and gossiping about others just for being who they are? Though we may not receive a standing ovation when we take a courageous stand and present our authentic selves, the act is no less heroic. And in the end, because it takes so much energy to put up a façade, it is much easier to just be ourselves!

> "DO YOU WANT TO BE A POWER IN THE WORLD? THEN BE YOURSELF."
> —RALPH WALDO TRINE

## POWER PRACTICES

- In what type of situations do you feel most congruent? In which do you tend to slip into inauthenticity?

- Can you think of a time you took a risk and spoke your truth? What did that feel like and what was the reaction to your truth?

# CHAPTER 36
## PATH OF TRUTH

Why do we lie? We think people cannot handle the truth. We fear loss of respect and the judgment of others. We fear not having the right answer, being thought of as stupid, losing face, not looking good. We feel shame about having to confess something we have done or failed to do. Underneath all of that is the fear of rejection. Remember, these are all the fears of the ego.

That's the bad news—the ways of the world, the human condition. Each time we tell a lie we diminish our personal power. We fraction ourselves off a little more. It is as if we had to create a different compartment in our minds to remember what we said to whom and not get caught in a lie. Like Sir Walter Scott's "tangled web we weave when first we practice to deceive," lies take a life of their own and require ongoing maintenance. Maintaining the illusion of a lie takes valuable effort and mental energy (mind power) that could be much better spent in other areas of our lives.

The word *integrity* stems from *integer*, as in "whole number." Telling the truth is about more than morality or religious commandments. Even more importantly, as far as I am concerned, it is about wholeness: achieving and maintaining personal integrity.

The good news is that every time we tell the truth in spite of whatever discomfort it might cause, we increase our personal power. Not only that, taking a stand for the truth in the present is like a time fuse into the past, healing previous similar situations in which we were unable to do so. To paraphrase Maia: We can all eventually come around to handle the truth, any truth. What we cannot handle are the lies.

Deceit and manipulation in the form of half- or withheld truths will often backfire. They cause resentment and breed mistrust, sometimes irreparably damaging and impairing our relationships.

In the Soulful Relationships retreats we elaborate on the practice of "clearing the space," which is imperative no matter how insignificant of a pebble a lie—or a withheld communication—may seem. If, like a garden, we have individual and common spaces where relationships can unfold, even tiny untruths take hold like weeds and begin to fill the common areas. Eventually there is no space left and the relationship withers. Part of cultivating our garden entails weeding and maintaining that common space to be open and clear. We will explore this more deeply in the next book of the series, *Attracting and Nurturing Relationships That Work*.

Sometimes we agree to do something when we have no intention of ever doing it in order to be nice or avoid conflict. We then waste precious mental energy feeling guilty about it, throwing out decoys or avoiding the person involved. Even though lying may not have been our intent, not keeping our word damages trust and relationships. Every time we say we will do something and don't, our power is diminished.

Sometimes the conflict is internal, as when I tell myself I'm going to organize my desk or office or the garage. But when months, maybe even years later, it is still a mess, I've lost credibility with myself; I begin to doubt my own word. In larger situations, others begin to doubt my word. Either way, that is a sorry state of affairs. Speaking the truth and learning to say no are powerful skills.

If we are already caught in a situation from the past, a much cleaner and more powerful way to handle that is to simply and formally unchoose it. The catch, though, is that in order to free ourselves. we have to communicate that. We have to pick up the phone and call our friend and say, "You know when I said I would help you do XYZ? I love you and value our friendship, but I am sorry; I'm not going to do that. How else can I help?" Though this may bring up immediate conflict, it is better to address the situation head on and keep the space clear, ultimately freeing both parties involved.

Being truthful to ourselves may be the most challenging, as it entails sifting through the filters, veils, and decoys of the ego. Blind spots are by definition that: places we can't see. This is one of the benefits of having Power Partners on the path to soulful power, and the reason why joining the Facebook Group or creating your own Power Pod can be helpful and supportive.

One important aspect of telling the truth connected to self-expression involves being who we are fully, not hiding parts of ourselves in order to attain the illusion of acceptance or maintaining peace. Standing up for ourselves, for our truth, requires courage. Sometimes there will be pushback, possibly repercussions. We might even be concerned about the survival of a relationship. If that happens, try to recall Maia's powerful story of congruence.

"TRUTH IS POWERFUL AND IT PREVAILS."
—SOJOURNER TRUTH

The world aligns around the truth. However, this does not mean we will always get a standing ovation when we take a stand for our beliefs. Sometimes we face the real possibility of rejection. Yet that is a chance soulful heroes are willing to take. We have to live with ourselves and face the mirror each morning—after, hopefully, sleeping peacefully at night.

When I decided to leave my life in Miami to join the ashram, my family and friends, many of whom thought I was crazy or feared I was joining a cult, freaked out. One guy in particular stands out. For years he had been singing my praises to the four winds that I was his "best friend" who had "saved his life" when I helped him navigate a painful separation. What makes the story even more interesting is the fact that he felt he had been wronged and victimized by his society friends, almost of all of whom had shunned and abandoned him when he came out as a gay man. In other words, he had been rejected for being his authentic self, for following his heart. Yet in the face of my decision, he judged me harshly and rejected me for doing just that—following my heart. When I went to collect money owed to me, my so-called friend kicked me out of his office, whipped out his wallet, and threw $200 cash at my feet. Was he feeling rejected—or fearful? Did my courage shame him because he wasn't able to make such a leap? I don't know for sure, but for many reasons, his ego likely shouted at him the same way he shouted at me.

So yes, rejection is a risk we take. Not every one of our relationships will take a leap with us. What we know, though, is that if a relationship does not survive then it was not a true one to begin with. In my case, those relationships that were true weathered the storms of change and are still here thirty years later. To adapt one of Maia's sayings ("What is in the mind of God will be there on the other side of the process of transformation"):

> WHAT IS TRUE, WHAT IS OF LOVE, WILL BE THERE ON THE OTHER SIDE OF THE LEAP.

The other thing to keep in mind is that when we take such a dramatic stance in the face of the ways of the world, we are actually threatening consensus reality. My simple act of walking away from a successful and in many ways enviable life was a threat to some people's status quo; their values and choices were possibly being brought into question in their own minds, at least subconsciously.

Speak only the truth. Lying eats away at our personal power. Great freedom lies simply in being our authentic selves.

## POWER PRACTICE

- What is one untruth that comes to mind that is occupying priceless real estate in one of your relationships? Pick first one that is not the scariest or the most challenging. What do you need to do clear the space and clean it up? What correction in the situation do you need to make? Maybe it's not something that needs to be said; perhaps you only need to show up differently or more authentically.

# CHAPTER 37
## PATH OF LETTING GO

The word *sacrifice* comes from the Latin *sacer* ("sacred, holy") and *facere* ("to do, perform"). In other words, to make holy. In the context of this book, we are sacrificing—making holy—our lives in service to something greater.

So, what exactly are we sacrificing? We are letting go of playing small, holding back, fear, limitation, anything that has held us back from living life at full throttle, at maximum capacity (power). We are letting go of the smallness and pettiness of the ego, its machinations, strategies, desires, opinions, and attachments—to people, places, ideas, beliefs, perceptions that no longer serve us. We are letting go of attitudes and situations that interfere with our inner peace, soulful power, and personal freedom.

We are letting go of:

- Being right. As long as we are holding on to being right and holding the other person to task for hurting us, we keep ourselves separate and stuck in tired patterns of victimhood.

- Expectations. We free ourselves and others to be however we/they want to be in any given situation. We retain choice as to how and if we want to be in close relationship with anyone. We release expectations about the way things are or "should" be.

- Judgment. Judging imprisons us as much as those we are judging. Underlying is a feeling of self-righteousness: we are right, and they are wrong. As we already saw with the mechanism of projection, at a deeper level we are making wrong in others some aspect of ourselves that we cannot accept. When we practice extending forgiveness—giving room to be human and less than perfect, we break these chains. We set ourselves—and others—free from the heavy weight and responsibility of having to be perfect or being right all the time. What pressure! How imprisoning!

- Conditioning. We identify and release layers of conditioning, the mores and beliefs about what is right, good, and appropriate that we have inherited from family and culture. We undertake the heroic and important work of questioning, and deciding that for ourselves.

- Limited thinking. We give up our belief that there is not enough of fill-in-the-blank in ourselves and others.

- Attachment. We release attachment to people, situations, things we think we *must* have in order to be happy, whether that is 100 pairs of shoes, a particular kind of car, our daily latte. Not that there is anything intrinsically wrong with any of these things! It is the attachment that binds us, as Buddhism teaches. Freedom is the goal. A note about clutter: As above, so below. Our outer space reflects our inner one. Yikes! That's the scary news. The good news is that as we organize our outer space, which is easier to do, our inner one will also reflect increased clarity, liberated attention, creativity, and efficiency. We will attain better results faster and more easily. We also relinquish attachment to outcomes—that things turn out a certain way—and to being in control. That's a big one! Instead, we simply show up. We give it our best. We release expectations and attachment to outcome. That is freedom. Make-wrongs, perceived failures, and self-punishment are not necessary.

We simply glean as much learning as possible from our past experiences for the purpose of growth and evolution.

- Identities. We let go of old and tired ways of seeing ourselves that no longer serve. Some years ago at a letting-go ritual at one of my retreats, I let go of an old identity that I was shy, which may have protected me at some point in my life when I was afraid of rejection and intimidated by social situations. I can still keep my identity of being introverted, which is a different dynamic. It means that I process things internally before speaking them, rather than figuring out what I mean or believe as I am speaking. Identity development is one area in which planned obsolescence is desirable. We continually shed those we have outgrown and, like a software program, release new and better versions!

- Stress. Cultivating our gardens—even "saving the world"— does not have to be done breathlessly, obsessively, and compulsively. We are giving birth to and taking a stand for a new world in which peace and balance begin within, a world in which we each declare ourselves a Universal Peace Zone.

That means we commit ourselves to cultivating inner peace, a process that has to be tended to, worked at. How will we choose to act when we get cut off in traffic? How will we choose to respond when we get a really rude customer-service representative on the phone after navigating automated voicemail limbo for 20 minutes? Or when we get home tired and cranky, and the kids are screaming and have made a huge mess in the living room and the new puppy peed on the couch? How will we choose to be when the boss unfairly yells at us for the delay or failure of a project, or when we are feeling overwhelmed and have no idea how we are going to make ends meet at the end of the month?

How do we do that? By reframing our thinking and taking on some kind of meditation practice. These help us get off the merry-go-round for at least a few minutes each day.

One of my favorite modern-day parables is told by Richard Bach in *Illusions: The Adventures of a Reluctant Messiah*. He tells of a race of little creatures living at the bottom of a river. Always subject to the river's relentless current, they survived by grabbing on to stones, twigs, or branches at the river bottom. There they lived in the mud at the mercy of the current and passing debris, "for clinging was their way of life and resisting the current what each had learned from birth." Eventually one of the creatures tired of his life and announced that he was going to let go, because if he didn't, he would "die of boredom." Mocking him, but more than likely terrified inside, the others warned him: "Fool! That current you worship will throw you tumbled and smashed across the rocks, and you will die quicker than boredom!" But the creature had had enough of his meaningless existence. He let go. Sure enough, at first, he was tossed and tumbled and thrown against stones, but eventually the current lifted him up and steadied him. The creature was liberated from his fearful, clinging existence; easily and gracefully he floated downstream, at one with the current, as if he were flying. Eventually, he drifted over another village of creatures who had never seen one of their kind do anything but hold on for dear life at the river bottom. Looking up in awestruck amazement, they called out "See, a miracle! A creature like ourselves, yet he flies. See the Messiah, come to save us all!" The creature responded, "I am no more Messiah than you. The river delights to lift us free, if only we dare to let go. Our true work is this voyage, this adventure!" And then he was swept away, leaving the others to make up elaborate stories about their savior.

Let go. That's what heroes do.

## POWER PRACTICES

- What is one thing you are you ready to let go of today? Is there an attachment to a specific outcome that comes to mind? An old identity you are ready to sacrifice? A limiting belief? Create a ritual for yourself. For example, write it down on a piece of paper and burn or bury it.

- What practices will you take on as you declare yourself a Universal Peace Zone? How will you cultivate inner peace? Formal sitting meditation? A regular walk in nature? Breathwork, perhaps? Attending a weekend retreat? Make your commitment specific—and keep it doable. How often will you commit to practicing? For how long?

# CHAPTER 38
## PATH OF SURRENDER

What a seeming conundrum. How can surrendering result in empowerment? It seems as though that means giving up our power to another. I suppose it is like a Zen koan, a riddle transcending logic and rationality that the mind will never understand using normal thinking processes—a mind-fuck, if you will.

Surrendering means letting go of the identification with the ego, or lower self, and reidentifying with another part of ourselves. We align ourselves with our higher nature, which some call the Higher Self, soul, or spirit. That part of who we are—the stadium—that is an aspect of the Godhead, Source. In effect, then, we are surrendering to ourselves. Which does not necessarily make it any easier!

Surrender can be an exquisite experience. It is as if we have been struggling, exerting ourselves swimming upstream against the current, unsuccessfully trying to avoid all sorts of hazards and obstacles, until we reach the moment when we say, "Enough! Can't do this anymore." We let go and allow the current to gently turn us around. Life becomes much easier. It becomes much more of an adventure lived moment to moment. The magic, for lack of another word, the synchronicities, the surprises become commonplace and undeniable.

Surrender is far from a passive state. It is active and proactive, creative and co-creative. It is not as though we suddenly shirk responsibility for our choices and turn over our free will: "Here, you do it!" On the contrary, we assume a higher level of responsibility. Our will becomes one with Divine will, and we assume a more active role in supporting creation.

When we surrender, we plug in to and access an inexhaustible power supply. We are surrendering to the Force, the life force that animates the Universe, the all-pervasive intelligence, the life-giving energy that forms and informs existence, the fabric and DNA of the cosmos—also known as God in some circles.

There is freedom in surrender. We retain free will every step of the way. It is not so much a directive but rather, a conversation, a dialogue, although we certainly can get the occasional "Do this!" In most cases it feels like a pleasant dialogue: "What do you want to do? No, what do *you* want to do?" It can be fun and funny.

Surrender is a process. Often, there is a significant moment followed by slighter more subtle gradations along the way. I got my first taste of surrender back early in 1990, just a few months after I had taken "A Call to Greatness" and begun doing breathwork and studying with Maia. It was at a day-long retreat on Easter, at which maybe 25 of her students had gathered at a retreat venue owned by the Catholic Church. Midway through the morning, a priest happened to look in the room. Seeing everyone dressed in white while chanting in Sanskrit and a Buddha statue gracing the altar, he promptly returned with the venue rental fee and asked us to leave. A short time later, having reconvened in someone's living room, we renewed our discussion about willingness. At one point Maia asked if anyone present was so ready to seek freedom, enlightenment, to follow their calling, that they were willing to do *whatever* that would take. With my heart palpitating in my mouth I raised my hand. She looked at me for a while, and then proceeded to interrogate me, each time raising the bar a little higher. "So, you would be willing to quit your job? Sell your condo? Leave Miami? End your relationship? Leave your family?" Each time my answer was the same: "Yes." I was freaking out at one level, but underneath the fear I felt the strange confidence of readiness. The level of "crisis" was palpable in the room as others silently contemplated their own responses to those questions. She let me stew in my juices overnight. First thing the next day one of her assistants called to emphasize that she was talking about willingness; she wanted to make sure I was not going to quit my job that day.

Even knowing that the dialogue was theoretical, I had a sense that, at least in my case, that level of declaration would not go untested. The moment would come when I would be given the opportunity to show myself—and the Universe—to what degree those yeses were real.

Three months later I was on a plane, having delivered on every one of those yeses. The job part was easy—it was no longer fulfilling or even appealing—although I certainly experienced fear of the unknown: How would I support myself? Letting go of the condo, car, and belongings was more difficult. Breaking up with my boyfriend was not easy. Though we loved each other, the truth was that I had known for some time that we were in different stages in our lives and growing in different directions. We were not a match. Saying goodbye to friends was also difficult, but the hardest test for me was leaving my family. I had gone away for college and had lived on my own for years since my return, but this was different. As I sat on the plane looking out the window at the shrinking city below as the plane U-turned away from the Atlantic Ocean and headed west, I had no idea when I would see them again. I pondered what my life would be like, how I'd survive financially, whether I would handle the rigorous demands of ashram life. Not the least of my concerns was the year of celibacy to which I and the five other disciples had committed—and I mean complete celibacy, which included my "five best friends" with whom I had had a constant intimate relationship since age ten.

As it turned out, I saw my family again within the year, and we were able to stay in regular contact—though strained at first—by mail and telephone. Around that time, I officially came out to my parents. (All my siblings already knew.) The level of honestly and congruence in our relationship was on the rise. For months though, I grieved leaving them behind.

In spite of all the demands and hardships of ashram life and all the freedom, comforts, and pleasures of my life which I had renounced, the hardest thing—hands down—of the whole experience was the day-to-day surrendering to the guru. The way it works is that the guru represents the Divine, thereby giving the disciple a more immediate and tangible experience than surrendering to a more abstract deity. At least once a day, and often more, for five years I surrendered my preferences, my will, my desires, even my perceptions to God, through the person of the guru. Those years were almost unbearably difficult. At times it was impossible for me to surrender, and I reacted with the hopeless rage of a caged animal. One time I shocked myself when, after a particularly frustrating telephone conversation with Maia, I picked up the phone and hurled it against the wall—something I had never done before and haven't done since.

Complicating matters was that I began to notice her behavior, to me at least, was at times irrational—emotional outbursts, apparent blind spots, things that did not fit my perception of how a guru behaved. Yet knowing about the ego's judgments and expectations, and knowing that the guru/disciple relationship was designed to help burn through the ego, I tried not to second-guess the process and stuck it out. After a while, she had begun to lose credibility to me as my guru, but I was so passionate about the value of her teachings that I remained committed to bringing them to the world. By this time, I had become her right- and left-hand person, publisher, publicist, events coordinator, heir apparent, substitute son—a very complex and multilevel relationship. I felt responsible not only for her getting her work out but also for her well-being in this realm. And of course, there were beautiful, amazing, wonderful times as well, and a wealth of exquisite, inexplicable, transcendent, and ecstatic moments, all yielding accelerated spiritual growth. Disentangling myself became increasingly difficult. I knew that when I left the whole thing would implode, which is what eventually came to pass. Years later Maia would renounce the role of teacher and guru.

For me, for whom being right was one of my strongest ego traps, those years remain the most challenging I have experienced to date. Among the emotions I frequently felt: Frustration. Despair. Trapped. Betrayed by God. Anger. Rage. Despondency. Hopelessness.

And yet, little by little my surrender deepened as my ego continued to get overridden. Poor thing: it was living in a constant state of psychological survival and overwhelm. But it paid off. At some point I began to realize that the hierarchical nature of the guru/disciple relationship was interfering with my own growth. There I was teaching people how to be free, and I did not feel free. By the time I found the right opportunity to leave her company, I had shown myself without a shadow of a doubt that yes, I was willing to do whatever it took, and to let it all go. Knowing that was priceless. As a matter of fact, the entire experience was just that, and I remain infinitely grateful. I would not be who I am today if it were not for that. Her teachings are still resonant and alive, even though the later years were difficult. And through me they have affected countless other lives.

And I continue to surrender. Years later, I was blessed with a partner who had the skills, training, and willingness to do the work of using our relationship as a laboratory for growth, a process on which we will focus in the next installment of the *Calling All Heroes* series, *Attracting and Nurturing Relationships That Work*. I was able to work on flattening the "being right" button (which was strong enough to survive the ashram experience!). I learned that even when I was right (which, for the record, I almost always was!), it mattered not one bit. As long as I had a charge or an investment on that, I was letting my ego win.

In the process of surrender—and in life—the external signs make it interesting and provide relief and confirmation that we are not going crazy. Timely, unexpected phone calls, a song on the radio with the perfect message, even literally, signs.

Years later, after being guided (tricked is more accurate) to leave my beloved Northern California and return to South Florida, I was going back and forth between Miami and Key West.

The former made more sense in that I would be more accessible to people and closer to major airports; Key West, on the other hand, provided more of a writer's retreat, a sense of escaping from civilization, a buffer from my past.

Then the guidance came that it was to be Miami, much to my surprise. That was not what I had signed up for nor what I wanted. Yet, after a year of traveling the country and waiting for signs, they were finally there, clear and undeniable. I said, "All right, all right, I'll do it!" I began "ambivalating" between a larger house in Miami with a beautiful, expansive meeting space—the reason for being there—and another smaller and less expensive one in the Keys that was more retreatlike and conducive to writing, but nowhere near as suitable for groups. One day as I was driving, I kept going back and forth in my mind between the two when suddenly, it was as if my head was being turned by the chin to look at a billboard. I must have passed it two dozen times in the previous few weeks without seeing it. The sign read: "Think Big!"

This example also illustrates how we know the difference between the desires and goals of the ego and the inclinations of the Higher Self. My ego certainly did not want to go back to Miami. Furthermore, it was overwhelmed by taking on the responsibility of a big house, the rent for which alone was twice what I had paid before. I felt it would tie me down in more than one way. In contrast, the Soulful Self bounced ideas off a couple of trusted advisors, calmly read the signs, and when these became clear and irrefutable, it signed the lease with the poor ego not quite kicking and screaming but still worried in the background. Now years later, it has all worked out and the Miami temple—both this house and its current iteration—has touched many a life and has provided me with a much-needed base and beloved sanctuary.

More recently I experienced a deeper level of surrender. The only thing that could have snagged me this lifetime was sex. Because of an early incident of sexual abuse, I was precociously awakened to sexuality, which became an intrinsic part of my life and identity even as an adolescent. I recently arrived at a place in life where I now know that if I had to let it go because it interfered with my spiritual evolution, I could do that, and would be OK with it. Thankfully, I don't think that is being asked of me, and I have no desire to be celibate again, as I was during my ashram years. But for the first time in my life I feel free in regard to sexuality. (We will explore sexuality—and celibacy—more deeply in Book 2.) What a powerful feeling—to know that I am free and can walk away from any aspect of my life if necessary. Such a pervasive sense of peace and power that generates. Surrender is the ultimate heroic act, and yet it's so natural. Sweet surrender. Empowered surrender.

> "THE GREATNESS OF
> A MAN'S POWER IS
> THE MEASURE OF HIS
> SURRENDER."
> —WILLIAM BOOTH

## POWER PRACTICE

- Create a ritual for yourself. For example, write down something (or a list of things) you are ready to surrender—a belief, a behavior, or some aspect of your life that you may have outgrown. Dispose of it with intention by burning, burying, or offering it to the ocean. Please be aware that letting-go rituals can be powerful and catalytic. In our retreats, it is so touching to see people releasing old stuff that has been holding them back; sometimes they struggle with their grief and the let-go to the point of tears. I've often heard them use these powerful experiences as reference points in their lives: "That was when I really let go of XYZ." These rituals are powerful!

# CHAPTER 39
## CONCLUSION: THE JOURNEY CONTINUES

As we have seen, because the ego is designed to keep us safe, we are hardwired to avoid risk. The price we pay for that is stuckness, complacency, mediocrity. Too often, too many of us refuse the call to adventure. We allow stuff to get in the way of our transformation and fulfillment: Excuses. Laziness. Procrastination. Distraction (social media, TV, the drama of others' lives).

And yet the still, quiet voice persists. The Great Adventure keeps beckoning us. The Call won't leave us alone. Until we respond, the state of ambivalence tends to create inner conflict. As time passes, that intensifies, and either the discomfort becomes so pronounced that we finally are compelled to act, or tragically, too often self-medication is the only way to ignore it.

But it's never too late, AND, our time here is brief. Act now. Say yes again. Take the next step. Answer the next call. The beautiful thing is that once we say yes, the path reveals itself. There's no one way to fulfill it. That's the beauty of the journey of exploration. And you can't mess it up. It is alive and by nature flexible. It will continue revealing itself. One step into the void, and then the stone shows up to meet us, as it did for Indiana Jones.

## The Adventure Continues

Congratulations! You have completed Book 1 and made your way through the Empire of the Ego and the Zone of Power. You now have a deeper understanding of who you are, how the ego mind works, how it cheats all of us of our potential and keeps us playing small. And now that you better understand the ego's shenanigans and machinations, you can more readily avoid getting trapped in power struggles that seldom end well or get you what we all really want: lives of meaning and purpose, happiness, relationships that work.

On the path to soulful power you have gone through the process of looking under the hood and deconstructing beliefs and assumptions about power. You have explored the pitfalls of power and the power plays we have all employed to get what we want or manipulate a situation.

You've seen the differences between worldly power and soulful power and have the tools to resolve any ambivalence about stepping into power. You now see that you can own your power; have clear boundaries; communicate your desires, your likes and dislikes, what works for you and what doesn't without fear of abusing power or causing harm. So, no more excuses!

The Power Practices are intended to support the process of reconnecting with and giving expression to your soulful power. It's a journey, a practice. As with anything else, the more we practice, the better we get. Then we become established at the next level of mastery. Going forward, you may slip and find yourself saying yes when inside you mean no, but it will happen less frequently. And you will learn to avoid or better navigate those frustrating power struggles.

This journey is heroic work, the work of a lifetime. Are you ready for more? In the next book we visit the Realm of Relationships, where we will explore how the ego and issues around power affect the arena of relationships, which is where most of us experience power leakages. For now, enjoy a sample chapter at the end of this book to give you a taste of what's coming.

If you accepted the call, embarked on the journey described in this book, and especially, if you actively engaged with the Power Practices along the way, you have been in the midst of a heroic journey, an adventure in transformation. Thank you! Your courage and willingness are nothing short of heroic—and they make a real difference in the world.

The adventure continues . . .

## POWER PRACTICES

- Go back to the initial list of heroic acts on pages 4–6 and review them from your current perspective. How many have you taken on during the journey this book provided? Which will you take on as an ongoing practice?

- On a scale of heroism from 1 to 10, where would you place yourself today? How does that number compare with how you answered that same question back on page 22? Are you able to see and own that you are a hero now, with greater clarity and certainty than you did at the onset of your journey?

- Please acknowledge your heroism by doing something nice for yourself this week . . . and share a picture of it on the Facebook Group!

## A MYTH FOR OUR TIMES

In these times of dramatic social change and collapsing structures, it can be easy to succumb to feelings of fear and hopelessness. The work of ethnobiologist Elisabet Sahtouris provides a beautiful framework and powerful context for our times.

Sahtouris spent years studying the transformational process of caterpillar into butterfly, uncovering what she named imaginal cells. Because these contain the DNA of the butterfly, which is slightly different than that of the caterpillar, the immune system of the latter views them as foreign objects and destroys them, the same way it would a virus or bacterium. Similarly, we could say that humanity has done the same to our prophets, light-carriers, and truth-speakers—the Jesuses, Gandhis and Dr. Kings: they pop up and we shoot them down.

At some point in the life cycle of the caterpillar, an internal mechanism is triggered, and it goes into a hyper-eating phase, engorging itself, eating everything around. In a way, humanity is doing the same, carelessly devouring our natural resources without regard even to our own survival on this planet.

There's an upside, however. In the case of the caterpillar, the hyper-eating phase also triggers a hyper-production of imaginal cells. Suddenly, these are popping everywhere, and they start gravitating toward each other, coalescing into imaginal clusters. Once they come together, the immune system of the caterpillar can no longer destroy them. It tries and tries until it fails, giving up, imploding into a mush, a nutrient soup that is what the imaginal cells feed on as they transform into the butterfly.

One could say that is where humanity is now. Systems are failing all around us, disintegrating in front of our eyes. The global economy is one breath away from collapse. The corporate, political, and church scandals have revealed the man behind the curtain.

We are the imaginal cells, awakening now to our full potential, no longer willing to live lives of frustration, lies, and mediocrity, or to hide our light under a bushel. Once we find each other and come together, we can no longer be destroyed.

What exquisite butterfly humanity transforms into—and whether we survive the metamorphosis—is yet to be seen. For the awakening imaginal cells, the call has gone out: to shine, to be more than we have ever been before, yes, even more than we can now imagine, to heal ourselves and become beacons for other imaginal cells, to come together and discover what we may do together that we can't do isolated and alone.

The mission is clear. Will you answer the call? Will you help us reach other imaginal cells?

NOTE: In gratitude for your having undertaken this journey, following is a link to a visual guided meditation about the imaginal cells. https://soulfulpower.com/just-keep-breathing/

## NEXT STEPS ON THE SOULFUL HERO'S JOURNEY

### Community

As you probably noticed, the heroic journey described here will take you through peaks and valleys, traps and quagmires, challenges and opportunities. Know that you are not alone. Beyond the realm of the ego you will find freedom and an ever-expanding tribe of awakening heroes. Connect. Reach out. Let's explore what we can do together that we couldn't do separate and alone. For a sense of community and support in the journey, make sure you join our free Facebook group: Unleash Your Inner Hero. Having the support of a broader community of fellow travelers will make all the difference during challenging times in the journey. Hopefully, you chose a smaller Power Pod for the journey, as the more intimate group is great for accountability and inspiration. There you will encounter others also committed to their journey of self-discovery and liberation.

### Repeat or Deepen Practices

Choose to deepen your Power Practices. This can be done either on your own, if you are more of a solitary journeyer, or with the support and camaraderie of other Soulful Heroes on your Power Pod or the Facebook group. For example, find someone else to forgive, or drop off another anonymous gift on a park bench. Keep it going. There are always deeper layers and more subtle challenges on the hero's journey . . . and infinite treasures and rewards to discover.

## Power Project

Self-empowerment is not enough for a hero. Heroes are driven to make a difference. Do you have a power project? What issues are you passionate about? There are so many problem areas in our world, in our communities. What will you take on? In the Facebook group you can connect with others sharing similar interests and passion. Together we can make a real difference.

> "DO THE THING AND YOU WILL HAVE THE POWER."
> —RALPH WALDO EMERSON

## Hero Champions

Some of us are especially gifted at weaving connections. In these times, however, we are all called to fulfill that role and connect with others. Our power is in the numbers. Together we can overcome the entrenched power structures of fear and oppression. Our army's motto: *Amo ergo sum.* "I love, therefore I am." Become a Hero Champion, an advocate, ambassador—an imaginal cell recruiter. Help us spread the word and identify other heroes who are waiting to hear their call. Invite them to the Facebook group. Send them a link to where they can purchase a book. And please, take a couple of minutes and write a review on Amazon! Even a sentence or two can make a huge difference. Maybe it's your words that reach that dormant hero and help awaken their soul.

## Just Breathe!

To find someone in your area who facilitates breathwork, please write us at info@soulfulpower.com.

## Attend Live Events

To expedite the process of transformation, there is no substitute for receiving the teachings in a more personal and profound way in combination with breathwork. At the retreats, you will discover a deeper understanding of self through a clearer prism, and the multiple breathwork sessions are nothing short of miraculous. The descriptions at the end will help you find one that best suits your needs.

## Online Programs

As an alternative for those unable to attend a live event, our online programs also offer tremendous support. And they come with a bonus: Because the teachings are spread out over a longer period of time, participants experience better integration of the lessons. This setup also supports the practices of the hero's tasks for the same reason.

Finally, stay tuned for **Attracting and Nurturing Relationships That Work**! Coming Summer 2021!

# EXCERPTS FROM
## *ATTRACTING AND NURTURING RELATIONSHIPS THAT WORK*

### RIDING THE RELATIONSHIPS ROLLER COASTER

F ew things can take us to the heights of ecstasy and the depths of despair as quickly and as frequently as relationships. Few things knock us off balance as easily and disconcertingly. Few things capture our focus and consume our attention as completely. Entire industries exist for the purpose of enhancing the possibilities of love, sex, and relationships.

Love and relationships can make us feel as though we are on top of the world or plummet us into deepest doubt, darkest despair, and ruthless self-questioning, all in the space of seconds. They can make us hurt so bad that emotional pain becomes physical. There are interesting studies about a real heart problem called "Broken Heart Syndrome" that stems from loss, grief, and damaged relationships.

The more I interact with participants in retreats, workshops, and other settings, the more evidence I find for the premise that most of us give our power away in the context of romantic relationships. This is where I consistently witness otherwise successful and empowered people selling out on their power, too often just for a few crumbs of acceptance, validation, or pseudo-love. Otherwise self-defined and strong-minded individuals, who are established professionally and even spiritually, can lose their sense of self when it comes to intimate relationships. They forfeit their power to avoid being alone, for the illusion of love. Yet, such explanations provide only a partial answer, for these people often experience love and acceptance in other areas of their lives. Why are they not relinquishing their power elsewhere?

What is it about love relationships of the romantic variety that unhinge us so, that make us lose our minds and our center? Is it hormonal? A trick of nature? These answers seem insufficient, because the madness persists after the initial falling-in-love period, even in cases where we come to understand that this person may not be—and, in fact, often isn't—the best match for us. Clearly, this is not a rational process.

The mysteries of attraction and love have yet to be deciphered by our species. We seem to be at the effect of forces far beyond our control that ignore differences in age, gender, belief, class, education, ethnicity, or even sexual orientation. For example, recent research has explored the role of scent and hormonal influences in sexual attraction. When under the influence of the love energies, we cannot think clearly, as if we were inside a cloud or a bubble, under a spell, or experiencing momentary lapses of sanity.

Why do we lose our sense of self in relationships? The word *ecstasy* comes from the Greek *ek* which means "out of" and *stasis*, which relates to "standing." In ecstatic states we thus stand outside ourselves—our egos. We become one and experience a collapse of ego boundaries that gives us a taste of freedom; in the presence of our beloved, time stops. The past and future fall away at times, and we find ourselves in the eternal moment. Though it may be brief and elusive, we want more of that.

In the frenzy of love, our emotions are off and running. We get high, literally, on the ensuing rush of endorphins, the release of hormones into the system. We are blinded by love, or at least, lust. We do and say things that we may later regret. Feeling unbound from the normal and predictable flow of our lives, we can be blinded to the possible repercussions of our acts and may end up dishonoring our bodies, placing our health at risk, and perhaps our families, careers, and futures. Nothing else matters in those exquisitely dangerous moments when in the throes of love.

But our madness has its plus side. In this context of sexual/romantic relationships we often allow ourselves to be most open and vulnerable. We allow ourselves to be truly seen.

Navigating relationships consciously is not easy; it's the stuff of heroes. Yet, when we do, our process of healing and transformation is sped up dramatically. And our relationships have an actual chance at success!

Here is the problem, though: In this fundamental area of life that is deeply wired to core identity issues about survival and self-worth, we lack the clarity, context, and skills to have successful, fulfilling relationships that actually work. Our educational and religious systems have failed us. This is the kind of stuff that I majored in psychology in college hoping to understand—what makes us tick as human beings—and received very few insights of practical value in the process.

So, let's dive in and explore some of the reasons we have such difficulties with issues ranging from finding the right partners to developing relationships that actually work.

## TOP TEN RELATIONSHIP CHALLENGES

1. We approach relationships with unrealistic expectations—mainly, that they will fulfill us or make us happy—and with a constellation of often-unconscious beliefs and attitudes that interfere with our dreams and block our desires.

2. We sell out to relationships that are not a real match, suppressing ourselves in order to avoid conflict or maintain the illusion of acceptance, validation, and love.

3. We lack a greater context for relationships as an integral aspect of and as catalysts for our personal growth and spiritual evolution.

251

4. We confuse "falling in love"—the temporary, emotional, hormone-infused high—with the act and art of loving, the sacred work of relationship. Additionally, our culture of immediate gratification and the "grass is greener" syndrome contribute to our jumping in and out of relationships, often prematurely.

5. We lack understanding of the ego and its mechanisms that result in bruising battles of the egos as we get stuck in patterns of being right, projecting, blaming, attacking and defending, and feeling like victims.

6. We carry around unhealed wounds and unresolved traumas that rear their ugly heads time and time again in our relationships.

7. We struggle through busy and overscheduled lives that leave little room for nourishing our relationships.

8. We have few role models and support systems for conscious relationships.

9. We have little understanding of our emotions and few skills as to how to deal with them.

10. We have not been taught effective, graceful, empowered communication.

\* \* \* \* \* \* \* \* \*

## *AMO ERGO SUM*: THE POWER OF LOVE

Soulful power is ultimately about love. The call to power is a call to love, to radical love.

What does that mean? Of course, we are not talking about a saccharine, Hallmark, milquetoast kind of love, but the "grab the elephant by the balls" kind of love Hafiz, the 14th-century Persian poet, described. The kind of love that rocks the world: the heroic act of keeping our hearts open no matter what.

Love is not wimpy or airy-fairy. Love is fierce. Love is power. Love transcends all, including time and space.

Jimi Hendrix said, "When the power of love conquers the love of power then the world will know peace." Author Anodea Judith expands this concept and applies it to the evolutionary process of humanity: We are currently experiencing a leap in evolution from the "love of power" (based in the third chakra, the center of power) to the "power of love" (based in the fourth chakra, the heart center).

We are entering the age of the heart. What is now called for is a new motto for this new era in which *amo ergo sum* replaces Descartes's *cogito ergo sum.*

I am . . . not because I think, but because I love.

I don't believe in a punitive God or a Last Judgment. But if there to be such a thing and I were hired to produce that event, I would want to know how much—not whom—did you love.

We have no more time for playing it safe. Clearly, that does not mean being stupid or careless, setting ourselves up for abuse, failure, or rejection, or becoming doormats. It means taking charge, taking our lives into our hands.

This is not likely to happen on the couch watching TV or working sixty-hour weeks. We have to be willing to dive fully into our lives and take risks. So what if we get hurt again. We'll get over it and grow from it and emerge stronger and wiser. For every 100 times we have fallen, we have gotten up 101. We rise again, opening our hearts, no matter what.

Keeping the heart open, doing the hard work of loving, is not a path for the faint of heart. In fact, it is the stuff of heroes. As we have seen, *courage* comes from the French *coeur* for "heart." The heart cannot be closed selectively. It's like the iris of the eye or the shutter of a camera. We open or close it to allow more or less light in. Or love, in this case. If we close it to mom for what she did or dad for what he failed to do, or to the ex who cheated on us or the former boss who fired us, we close it. Period. Whenever we close it to any one person who hurt us, or to a group of people who look, think, believe, or love differently than we do, we are shutting off part of our heart.

This is the profound wisdom behind Jesus' radical teachings to "love your enemy." Literally, not metaphorically, we keep our hearts open, our heart centers, our energy centers, to everyone, no matter what.

We choose love. We let it be about love.

Our work is becoming hollow reeds for the cosmic force of love to flow through us. In her song "Trust Love," Rikki Byars reminds us that we are "givers and receivers of love." How simple is that? Our jobs are therefore laid out for us. How much love can we give and how much can we receive? That is our purpose, ultimately!

We are like vessels of love, infinite vessels. Our job is to keep the channels clear, removing obstacles, anything where it could get snagged. We become the hollow reeds the Buddhists talk about, through which love can flow freely.

We are love's keepers—not in a hoarding sense, of course, but as stewards. We tend to its needs. We become fluid. We become permeable to the substance of love, let it flow through us. We can never trap it or contain it, but we can be vessel for it. We keep ourselves clear and it will find us worthy. All we have to do is say "Yes" to love's call.

What would Love do?

I hope this gives you a taste of what's coming. Stay tuned! *Attracting and Nurturing Relationships That Work*! Coming Fall 2021!

# DEDICATION

This book is dedicated to three women who have profoundly influenced my life, and to one man. First, my mother, Raquel, from whom I learned to love deeply, unconditionally, holding nothing back. The courage and countless sacrifices she and my father Rene made so that their nine children could have a chance at freedom are nothing less than humbling, and a portrait in heroism.

Second, Maia Dhyan, my former spiritual teacher, who gave me the gift of breathwork and understanding of the ego—teachings and practices I have passed on now to countless others—and who provided the opportunity for a depth of surrender I may not have otherwise experienced.

And third, to P. L. Thorndike, who has been a faithful friend and steady supporter of my work in multiple ways, and who embodies and exemplifies a life filled with magic and sacred stewardship of the land. And because a deal is a deal, P. L., here it goes: to Alpaca Consciousness!

Last, I would like to honor my nephew Ralf Garcia, a true hero in the traditional sense. At 28, Rafi was diagnosed with a brain tumor and died ten days later, leaving behind his then seven-month pregnant wife (with their son, Mason).

The tragedy of Rafi's passing made international news and touched the hearts of many, not only because of the heartbreaking aspects of the story, but also because of the kind of man he was. The chief of the Miami Fire Department said in his comments at the funeral that normally when he speaks at such events, he reviews the personnel files. This time he didn't have to because he had already received eight unsolicited emails from Ralf's colleagues. That is part of his legacy—the love and respect he leaves behind.

Few experiences in my life have touched my soul as deeply. As one of his firefighter brothers said, Ralf was the type of person who genuinely appreciated something about everyone and always sought to find their best—and in the process inspiring people to be just that.

A couple of other lessons from the tragedy of his premature passing: Follow your passion, your dreams. My nephew turned down Harvard to follow his dream of becoming a firefighter/EMT. What dreams have you been postponing?

Give it your best. And give it your all. No more holding back or playing small. As his widow Maeghan wrote: "Ralf was the type of man who did everything all the way. When he made a decision, he saw it through to the end. He gave every endeavor his all. He gave me his all. He loved with every fiber of his being. I pray for God to give me the strength and ability to live and love that way. I pray I find the courage to continue to follow my dreams, and to fulfill the dreams we shared together.... Go out and love those around you without fear of getting hurt. When the person is worth it, the pain that sometimes follows is worth it, too."

Be a hero, your own kind of hero.

Let's seize the moment . . . and live full-assed.

# ACKNOWLEDGMENTS

As they say, it takes a village to raise a child—and to get a book published. My heartfelt gratitude and appreciation to:

Lynda McDaniel for her insightful editing. After living deep in the concepts and teachings for decades, it was an invaluable service to have someone with an outside perspective inspire me to dig deeper in order to better illustrate concepts. Beyond that, it's a blessing to find an editor who can help reorganize, rethink, or reword more clearly while always honoring the author's voice.

My beloved author friends who took the time to read the book and provide eloquent and powerful words of endorsement, thank you! I know how demanding all our schedules are. Your support is deeply appreciated.

Gloria Estefan, thank you for taking the time to read the manuscript. I have been a fan since the days Miami Sound Machine played at Belen High School dances. It's a privilege to witness the woman and the powerhouse you have blossomed into. Your talent, grace, and generosity have impacted countless lives, and the way you recovered from the bus accident inspires so many of us to find the courage and strength to overcome what can feel unsurmountable. That's the stuff of heroes!

Matthew Fox, astonishingly prodigious author, world-renown theologian, and spiritual revolutionary, whose book, *The Hidden Spirituality of Men: Ten Metaphors to Awaken the Sacred Masculine*, first inspired my thinking on what it means to be a man in the 21st century. It truly has been a privilege to witness your eloquence, brilliance, courage, passion, dedication, and humility over the years—and to be able to call you a friend and spiritual brother.

Robert Johanson, also my spiritual brother, for your invaluable perspective and suggestions, and for your steadfast encouragement over the years to finish this book.

Marjorie Van Dyke, my trustworthy, reliable, and crackerjack assistant and business manager, without whose support I would have never been able to complete the book while juggling multiple projects. That you for being able to both hold the big picture and help manage the details—especially during times of crisis.

Colby Smith, for your feedback, suggestions, presence, and support.

Rina Pal (Laizaa) for finding the right balance between "soulful" and "powerful" in the cover design; and Oscar Paludi and Maicol Arango, for your beautiful maps and illustrations.

Marc Gave, for your attention to detail and insightful, incisive proofreading.

Terry Anderson, for the last-minute rescue with Word formatting.

Without diminishing the horrible tragedy—the many deaths, the multilevel pandemic of human suffering, the heroic work by our healthcare providers and other essential workers, and the economic crisis that has ensued—I want to acknowledge my gratitude for being able to take advantage of the COVID-19 mandatory global time out to finish this book. I can't imagine how I could have ever finished it with the travel and event schedule I have been keeping for years.

# ABOUT THE AUTHOR

For more than thirty years, Christian de la Huerta has been dedicated to facilitating personal transformation. An award-winning author, Christian is a respected teacher and sought-after speaker whose unique self-development programs have been experienced across the world in university lecture halls, retreat centers, corporate boardrooms, and houses of worship. His role can be described in a variety of ways: retreat facilitator, relationships expert, spiritual coach, leadership consultant and beyond. While his dedication manifests in a variety of ways for a diverse audience, all of Christian's work shares a common result: profound personal transformation.

Christian is the creator and teacher of several self-development programs designed to help people get free and step into their authentic power in order to enjoy lives of meaning and purpose and relationships that work. His mission is to help catalyze a revolution of consciousness for the sake of humanity's evolution.

His award-winning book, *Coming Out Spiritually*, was chosen by *Publisher's Weekly* as one of the ten best religion books of its year. The book was widely regarded critically and is considered a defining, trendsetting accomplishment in its field.

Christian is an acclaimed speaker at various settings—including the TedX stage. He projects a compelling, authentic, and warm presence when speaking in front of groups, large and small. He speaks from experience and walks his talk, and audiences feel that—and find his message particularly relevant in these times. Over the years, he has established himself as a respected leader in the field of spirituality. His retreats, workshops and other events are known for their life-changing effect and for their inspiring and transformative exploration of our innate human potential.

Graduating with honors from Tulane University, Christian earned a degree in psychology. After working in the marketing and professional relations departments for several psychiatric and addictions hospitals in Miami, he walked away from his comfortable life to embark on a profound and challenging spiritual journey. Following a twenty-year period in the San Francisco Bay area, he again calls South Florida home, providentially finding his way back to Coconut Grove, his favorite Miami neighborhood.

More about his work may be found at www.SoulfulPower.com.

# ENDNOTES

1  Ken Wilber, *Up from Eden: A Transpersonal View of Evolution* (Boston: New Science Library, 1981), 7–8.

2  Peter Russell, "The Evolution of Consciousness," Peter Russell—Spirit of Now, https://www.peterrussell.com/SCG/EoC.php.

3  Helen Shucman, *A Course in Miracles: Text* (Tiburon, CA: Foundation for Inner Peace, 1985), 364–365.

4  IsanaMada, *A Call to Greatness: A Spiritual Journey of Self-Discovery and Self-Expression* (San Francisco: Dhyana Press, 1994), 210.

5  "Karma Chameleon, by Culture Club," SongFacts, https://www.songfacts.com/facts/culture-club/karma-chameleon.

6  Yehuda Berg, *Satan: An Autobiography* (New York: The Kabbalah Center, 2009), 34–36.

7  Helen Shucman, *A Course in Miracles: Manual for Teachers* (Tiburon, CA: Foundation for Inner Peace, 1985), 78.

8  James Hillman, *Kinds of Power: A Guide to Its Intelligent Uses* (New York: Currency Doubleday, 1995), 108.

9  "Commentary on Article XVIII – The Family," Southern Baptist Convention, The Baptist Faith and Message, June 14, 2000, http://www.sbc.net/bfm2000/articleXVIII.asp.

10 Kristen Wyatt, "Carter Cuts Southern Baptist Tie," *The Washington Post*, October 21, 2000. https://www.washingtonpost.com/archive/politics/2000/10/21/carter-cuts-southern-baptist-tie/.

11  Fiona Govan, "Vatican says women priests a 'crime against faith,'" *The Telegraph*, July 15, 2010, https://www.telegraph.co.uk/news/worldnews/europe/vaticancityand-holysee/7892666/Vatican-says-women-priests-a-crim e-against-faith.html.

12  Marianne Williamson, *A Return to Love: Reflections on the Principles of A Course in Miracles* (New York: HarperCollins, 1992), 190–191.

13  "Bullying Statistics," Bullying Statistics: Anti-Bullying Help, Facts, and More, accessed June 14, 2020, http://www.bullyingstatistics.org/content/bullying-statistics.html.

14  Viktor Frankl, *Man's Search for Meaning* (Boston: Beacon Press, 1959), 65–66.

15  American Psychological Association, January 7, 2019. https://twitter.com/apa/status/1082401926782861316?lan g=en.

16  National Institute of Mental Health, "Statistics: Suicide," accessed June 14, 2020, https://www.nimh.nih.gov/health/statistics/suicide.shtml#part_154969.

17  Henry Rollins, "Men are expected to be 'strong silent types'—and it's breaking them," *Los Angeles Times*. June 20, 2019, https://www.latimes.com/books/la-ca-jc-review-jared-yates-sexton-man-they-wanted-2 0190620-story.html?fbclid=IwAR0USLnk0duA8d16lf7C gdlCxmZkX5fKvBR8-Rbm_U6bxCKMqpA4_VazTpI.

18  Jared Yates Sexton, *The Man They Wanted Me to Be: Toxic Masculinity and a Crisis of Our Own Making* (Berkeley: Counterpoint Press, 2019), 8–9.

19  Mona Chalabi, "How Many Women Earn More Than Their Husbands?," Fivethirtyeight. February 5, 2015, https://fivethirtyeight.com/features/how-many-women-earn-more-than-their-husbands/.

20  Giffords Law Center, "Domestic Violence & Firearms," accessed June 14, 2020, https://lawcenter.giffords.org/gun-laws/policy-areas/who-can-have-a-gun/domestic-violence-firearms/.

21 Mark Follman, "Armed and Misogynist: How Toxic Masculinity Fuels Mass Shootings," *Mother Jones*, May/June 2019, https://www.motherjones.com/crime-justice/2019/06/domestic-violence-misogyny-incels-mass-shootings/.

22 Matthew Fox, *The Hidden Spirituality of Men: Ten Metaphors to Awaken the Sacred Masculine* (Novato, CA: New World Library, 2008), 19–32.

23 Matthew Fox, *Original Blessing: A Primer in Creation Spirituality* (Santa Fe: Bear & Co, 1983), 176.

24 "3 Man Killers: Power," The Art of Manliness, https://www.artofmanliness.com/articles/3-man-killers-power/.

25 Mary Kawena Puhui and Samuel H. Elbert, *Hawaiian Dictionary* (Honolulu: University of Hawaii Press, 1986), 340.

26 Alex Korb, PhD. "The Grateful Brain," *Psychology Today*, November 20, 2012, https://www.psychologytoday.com/us/blog/prefrontal-nudity/201211/the-grateful-brain.

27 World Bank, "Poverty Overview," accessed June 14, 2020, https://www.worldbank.org/en/topic/poverty/overview.

28 L.V. Clark, "Effect of mental practice on the development of a certain motor skill," *Research Quarterly*, vol 31 no 4 (Dec 1960):560–569.

29 A.J. Adams, "Seeing Is Believing: The Power of Visualization," *Psychology Today*, December 3, 2009, http://www.psychologytoday.com/blog/flourish/200912/seeing-is-believing-the-power-visualization.

30 Keith Ayers. "Elements of Trust," Integro Leadership Institute, https://keithayers.typepad.com/files/elements-of-trust.pdf.

31 "The 'Golden Rule' (a.k.a. Ethics of Reciprocity)," Religious Tolerance. http://www.religioustolerance.org/recip-roc2.htm.

32 IsanaMada, *A Call to Greatness*, 23–27.

# INDEX

# YOU'VE READ THE BOOK...

*Now Awaken Your Soulful Power!*

✓ JOIN OUR COMMUNITY!

✓ CHECK OUT OUR COACHING PROGRAMS

✓ ATTEND OUR LIVE RETREATS

Discover greater personal empowerment,
healthier relationships and a life filled with
meaning and purpose!

## Learn More

https://soulfulpower.com/AwakenYourSoulfulPower/
Info@SoulfulPower.com or (877) 773-7557

# *"Full of words to live by..."*

Praise for Christian's first book, *Coming Out Spiritually,*
chosen by Publishers' Weekly as one of the ten best
religion books of its year.

"Christian de la Huerta's book is an inspiring and ennobling look at our identities and purpose as LGBT people, and I recommend it highly ... The book is worth reading."

—The Los Angeles Times

"De la Huerta's beautifully crafted prose and his passionate desire to help LGBTQ people come out spiritually mark this book as an extraordinary achievement."

—Publishers Weekly

"Written inclusively and warmly, *Coming Out Spiritually* expands the lineage of those of us who comprehend gayness as comprising positive, transformative attributes of spiritual office. This is a book to treasure and teach. "

—Judy Grahn, Author of *Another Mother Tongue*

"*Coming Out Spiritually* is an encyclopedia of possibilities that make coming out politically and coming in spiritually easier and more joyous."

—Andrew Ramer, Author of *Two Flutes Playing and Revelations for a New Millennium*

"Coming Out Spiritually is comparable to Jean Shinoda Bolen's *Goddesses in EveryWoman* and Pinkola Estes' *Women Who Run with the Wolves*. It reveals how we may apply spiritual and archetypal wisdom relating to erotic and genered diversity to enrich our daily lives."

—Randy P. Conner, Author of *Cassell's Encyclopedia of Queer Myth, Symbol, and Spirit*

## *Order now on Amazon*

https://www.amazon.com/Coming-Out-Spiritually-Next-Step/dp/0874779669

# Soulful Hero Coaching

## WITH CHRISTIAN DE LA HUERTA

### EMBARK ON A HERO'S JOURNEY OF TRANSFORMATION

3-month
6-month and
Year-long programs

*"Christian is gifted with the ability to lovingly cut through surface shields and protections, powerfully evoking people's innate essence and inspiring their highest expression."*

## ARE YOU READY TO UNLEASH THE HERO WITHIN YOU?

Our coaching programs are for clients at all levels of personal transformation.

Christian is deeply committed to and passionate about working with you to bring forth your unique and extraordinary potential, to helping you step into your Soulful Power, creating a life that is tranformed into inspired living!

*In our inspiring self-empowerment programs you will learn to:*

- *Create a viable path that will help you discover a sense of belonging*

- *Develop a powerful sense of purpose and empowerment*

- *Feel energized, focused and motivated to share your soul's purpose with the world*

Learn More: https://soulfulpower.com/coaching/
Contact us at Info@SoulfulPower.com or (877)773-7557

# ARE YOU SURFING FOR LOVE IN ALL THE WRONG PLACES?

## Soulful Relationships Retreat
### WITH CHRISTIAN DE LA HUERTA

### WHAT ARE YOUR PERSONAL BARRIERS TO LIVING WITH A TRULY OPEN HEART?

Whether you are single or in relationship, and no matter how you express your love, come explore relationship as a vehicle for personal growth and spiritual transformation.

You will receive invaluable information and tools that make possible relationships that really work. You will emerge clearer, inspired, confident and more resolved and equipped to express yourself fully in relationships and in the world.

**You will learn to:**

• *Transcend obstacles to love and heal patterns of unhealthy relationships*

• *Use your relationships consciously to speed up your healing an transformation*

• *Evolve the way you hold relationships*

• *Discover deeper levels of personal fulfillment personally and in relationships*

### TOGETHER, WE'LL CRACK OPEN THIS JUICY QUESTION—AND BEGIN TO WORK TOWARD SOLUTIONS.

Learn More: https://soulfulpower.com/offerings/retreats/relationship-guidance/
Contact us at Info@SoulfulPower.com or (877)773-7557

# AWAKEN YOUR SOULFUL POWER!

## Soulful Power Retreat
### WITH CHRISTIAN DE LA HUERTA

## WHY MUST WE STEP INTO PERSONAL POWER CONSCIOUSLY, WITH INTENTION?

On a micro level, to avoid settling for a life of unfulfilled potential. On a macro level, because the world needs us—those of us who have an inkling that our work is to advance our collective evolution on this planet—as healers, teachers, activists and catalysts of change.

There has never been a more critical time in the history of humanity. The clarion call has been issued. The world needs us now. Come join us!

**Let's Power Up!**

*In this inspiring self-empowerment program you will learn to:*

- *Stop cheating yourself and playing small. Step into your role as an agent of change and world evolution!*

- *Heal your relationship to power and navigate conflicts with confidence*

- *Conquer insecurity and feelings of unworthiness so that you can unleash your soulful power in healthy and authentic ways*

Learn More: https://soulfulpower.com/offerings/retreats/soulful-power-soflo/

Contact us at Info@SoulfulPower.com or (877)773-7557

# UNCOVER YOUR TRUE PURPOSE: YOUR LIFE'S DEEPER MISSION

## *Soulful Purpose Retreat*
### WITH CHRISTIAN DE LA HUERTA

THE SOUL'S MESSAGE REVEALS TO US WHO WE ARE AND WHAT WE ARE HERE TO DO—GIVING MEANING, PERSPECTIVE AND SPIRITUAL INSPIRATION TO EVERYTHING ELSE

The soul speaks to us in many ways, often subtly and in ways our conscious minds find difficult to interpret. Yet of all the information we receive from the people and circumstances around us, the soul's message is by far the most important; it's one we simply must learn to understand.

These are just a few of the important questions we will explore together to help uncover what are you here to do at a soul or mission level: If money was not a consideration how would you spend your time? What turns you on spiritually? What kind of legacy do you want to leave behind?

**You will learn to:**

• *Gently yet powerfully open to your soul's message*

• *Explore techniques to integrate your soulful purpose into daily life*

• *Uncover fears and remove obstacles to realizing your true purpose*

• *Gain passion, confidence and clarity*

Learn More: https://soulfulpower.com/offerings/retreats/clarity-and-purpose/
Contact us at Info@SoulfulPower.com or (877)773-7557

# WHAT DOES IT MEAN TO LIVE HEROICALLY—IN THESE TIMES?

## Calling LGBTQ Heroes Retreat

### WITH CHRISTIAN DE LA HUERTA

## WHAT DOES IT MEAN TO COME OUT SPIRITUALLY?

People we today call lesbian, gay, bi, trans or queer have a long tradition of fulfilling spiritual roles such as teachers, healers, scouts of consciousness, mediators and keepers of beauty

We will explore these and other potent & important questions: Have you suspected that you had a role to play as teacher, healer or spiritual activist? How are you giving expression to those roles in your life? What role has LGBTQ people played throughout history?

*You will experience:*

- *Deeper levels of self-love and self-acceptance*

- *Soul-nourishing rituals and practices that will help you break through past limitations and unleash your true potential*

- *An expanded context for who you are and your importance to the world's evolution.*

- *Connection with other spiritual adventurers on a journey of self-discovery and empowerment*

Learn More: https://soulfulpower.com/offerings/retreats/a-call-for-lgbt-heroes-retreat/
Contact us at Info@SoulfulPower.com or (877)773-7557

# BREATHING INTO PURPOSE

## New Year's Retreat

### WITH CHRISTIAN DE LA HUERTA

DO YOU HAVE AN AMBIVALENT RELATIONSHIP TO YOUR
GREATER PURPOSE—YOU WANT IT BUT ARE AFRAID OF IT?

#### IT'S TIME TO STEP THINGS UP!

This empowering, inspiring and life-changing retreat will give you the support you need to go deep within, harvesting the lessons of the past year and bringing it to graceful completion—while launching the New Year with clarity of focus and powerful intention.

Together, we'll emerge grounded, renewed and connected to self and a sense of purpose from deep within.

**You will learn to:**

• *Uncover and identify your true purpose: your life's deeper mission*

• *Develop techniques and practices to build a life filled with meaning and purpose*

• *Heal unhealthy patterns and fears that hold you back from your calling*

Learn More: https://soulfulpower.com/offerings/retreats/new-years-retreat-breathing-into-purpose/

Contact us at Info@SoulfulPower.com or (877)773-7557

Made in the USA
Columbia, SC
07 October 2020

22288164R00178